About The Book

The purpose of writing "A Step by Step Guide to Book Keeping for Non Accounting Professionals" is to facilitate people who are working in the schools especially teachers who are performing additional duty of maintaining books of accounts for the institutions. We know, for some educational institutions, it is not possible to hire a separate person for the maintenance of school finances because these institutions are not financially strong enough or due to some other reasons.

In order to facilitate those people, this book is prepared in such way that will help them to understand what the book keeping is all about and how it is done.

The first good thing about this book is that it is written in easy and simple English so the non accounting/finance professionals can easily read and understand it. Moreover this book contains more practical work than the theory because book keeping is something which comes by practicing, "The more you practice, the better you understand".

The material used in this book is mostly used from the standard procedures of DBE to facilitate the teachers who are not only teaching in its schools but also engaged in the maintenance of schools' books of accounts because once they will practice the material used in the exercise it will help them to prepare their books of accounts on the same formats used in their standard books of accounts.

I would like to thank the Diocesan Board of Education Islamabad/Rawalpindi for providing me the opportunity and support to share my knowledge with the staff working in its school.

Contents

Part I
Understanding Book Keeping

Chapter One – Understanding Book Keeping

A book keeping is a process of recording financial activities (transaction) into books of accounts and comprises of following four basic steps:

Accounting Cycle

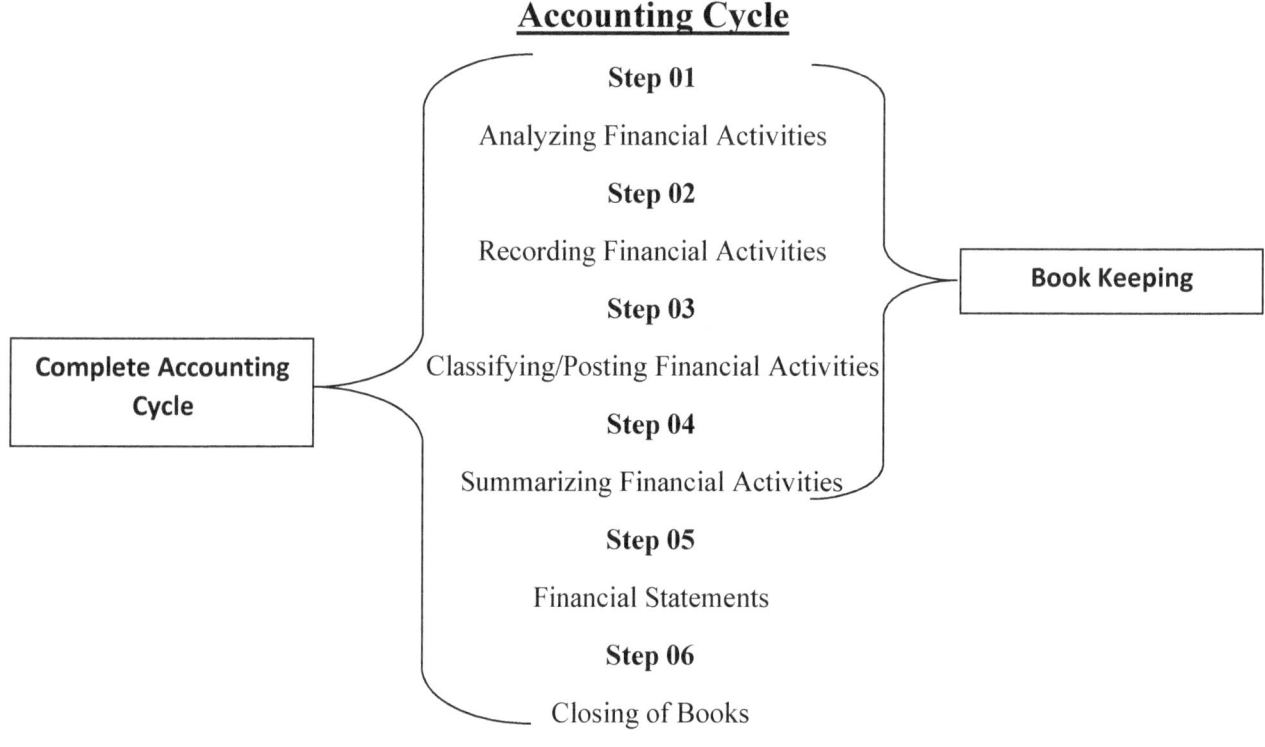

Step 01

Analyzing Financial Activities

Step 02

Recording Financial Activities

Step 03

Classifying/Posting Financial Activities

Step 04

Summarizing Financial Activities

Step 05

Financial Statements

Step 06

Closing of Books

Book Keeping

Complete Accounting Cycle

Step 01: Analyzing Financial Activity

In the first step, once the financial activity is performed, the nature of the financial activity is analyzed and examined what evidence are available to as a source document to support the nature of activity. It is recommended to get at least one source document in black and white.

For example:

Cash is received from Parent against tuition fee. To analyze this transaction, we need to check whether there is any documentary proof (Carbonated Fee Receipts etc.) that shows the amount received is against tuition fee. Carbonated Fee Receipts are the source document for the financial activity performed. Similarly, for a payment against an invoice / bill of stationery, we need to check whether the bill is with proper approval or the approval is needful to make it a proper source document. So in this case an invoice or bill of stationery along with its approval is considered a source document.

Step 02: Recording the Financial Activity/Transaction

Once we have analyze the financial activity and collected source document, then we are in a position to move to the next step which is recording a financial activity. Financial Activity (transaction) is normally recorded in the General Journal which is also called original book of entry but in order to lower the loud of transactions in the original book of entry different journals or books of entries have been introduced such as sales day book, purchase day book, cash receipt book or vouchers etc.

We will be working on mainly two types of vouchers or journals i.e., Cash (Cash in Hand and Cash at Bank) Receipt Vouchers and Cash (Cash in Hand\Cash at Bank) Payment Vouchers. We will use General Journal or General Voucher only if we need to make some adjustment entry in the School accounts.

For example:

Cash is received from Parent against tuition fee which is analyzed from the source document i.e., Fee Receipts. Instead of taking out each receipt from the receipt book, we should prepare a list of all the receipts collected in a day against tuition fee and related income and get it approved from the approving authority and use it as a source document with the receipt voucher and carbon copies of the receipts should be kept safe for verification purpose. After preparing the list or daily summary of fee income, we are required to prepare a cash receipt voucher in such a way:

Daily Fee Summary					
Date	Receipt No.	Admission Fee	Tuition Fee	Annual /Student Fund	Extra Student Charges

Particulars	A/C NO	Debit	Credit
Cash	XXX	XXXX	
To Tuition Fee	XXX		XXXX
Total		**XXXX**	**XXXX**

In case of Cash receipt vouchers, cash account is always debited whereas incomes against which cash is generated are credited. Sometimes cash is considered as income by most of the non commerce background people and since this book is mainly prepared for the people without any accounting background so it is highly recommended that they should not considered cash as income because in accounting cash is an asset.

Receipt Voucher (Cash\Bank)
Date : _____
Payee : _____   Voucher No
Rupees: _____   Cheque No.

Particulars	A\C No.	Debit	Credit
Total			

Prepared By   **Approved By**

It is also very much important that the debit side of the cash receipt or payment voucher should be equal to the credit side. Other details are also required on the vouchers i.e., Date, Payee, Voucher No., Cheque No. etc.

Similarly, for a payment against an invoice / bill of stationery, we need to get it approved to make it a proper source document. For approval we will be using some standard forms such as Expense form A (Approval for one type of Expense) and Expense Form B (Approval for more than one type of Expenses).

Expense form A
No.

Date:

Amount: _____   Cheque No. _____

To: _____   Acc No: _____

School/unit: _____

Description / Purpose: _____
_____
_____
_____

Approved by: _____   Received by: _____

EXPENSE FORM D.B.E.

Name:	B. Khan	School/unit:	Teacher inservice team		Date:	30-sep	
Date	Description	Petrol /Transport	Car	Stationary	Entertainment	Other	Total
11-sep	Tea with staff				85		85
14-sep	Flower for bishop					100	100
15-sep	Photocopies of training material			140			140
15-sep	Petrol 21.3 L. Km 85,360	644					644
16-sep	Replacing oil filter		120				120
18-sep	Photo film					100	100
20-sep	File tag			216			216
20-sep	Bus to Peshawar	65					65
20-sep	Taxi from busstand to St. John's	25					25
Total		734	120	356	85	200	1495

Receipts have to be attached

Checked by: Approved by: Received by:
                                          Date:

Once the source document is ready we will record the entry in cash payment voucher in such a way:

Particulars	A/C NO	Debit	Credit
Stationery Expense	xxx	xxxx	
To Cash	xxx		xxxx
Total		**xxxx**	**xxxx**

Here cash is always credited and all the expenses (reasons) against which cash is credited are Debited like stationery expense is debited and cash credited.

> Concepts on incomes/expenses and assets/liabilities/equity and their debit/credit recording effects are explained at the end of the book.

Payment Voucher (Cash\Bank)
Date : _____
Payee : _____   Voucher No
Rupees: _____   Cheque No.

Particulars	A\C No.	Debit	Credit
Total			

Prepared By   Approved By

Being experienced in training different non accounting background professionals, I would suggest instead of making them understand what are income/expense etc., concepts and recording treatments, we should provide them preprinted cash receipt and cash payment vouchers with unique numbers and give them some basic understanding of the concepts. It does not mean that we should not help them to understand the above mentioned concepts if interested.

Receipt Voucher (Cash\Bank)
Date : _____
Payee : _____   Voucher No
Rupees: _____   Cheque No.

Particulars	A\C No.	Debit	Credit
Cash	100		x
Bank	105		x
To Student Registration Fee	800	x	
To Admission Fees	801	x	
To Tuition Fees	802	x	
To Exam Fees	803	x	
To Misc. Charges	804	x	
To Annual/Student Fund	805	x	
To Income from Sales	806	x	
To Interest On Saving	807	x	
To Interest on Investment	808	x	
To Grants/Donations Congre	809	x	
To Grants/Donations DBE	810	x	
To Diocese Contribution	811	x	
To Other Donations	812	x	
To Income from Org. Activites	813	x	
To Other Income	814	x	
To Others	815	x	
Other	816	x	
		x	
		x	
Total			

Prepared By   Approved By

Payment Voucher (Cash\Bank)
Date : _____
Payee : _____   Voucher No
Rupees: _____   Cheque No.

Particulars	A\C No.	Debit	Credit
Teachers' Salary	500		x
Other Staff Salaries	501		x
Compulsory Contributions	502		x
Overtime Payment	503		x
Water/Electricity Expenses	506-7		x
Gas/Internet and Telephone	508-9		x
Rent/Insurance/S.S. Charges	510-2		x
Capital Building/Furniture	513-4		x
Capital Equipment/Vehicle	515-16		x
Repairs Building/Furniture	517-8		x
Repairs Equipment/Vehicle	519-20		x
Stationery and Printing Exp.	521		x
Postage and Revenue Exp.	522		x
Teaching Material	523		x
Office Expenses	524		x
Transportation Expenses	525		x
Training /News paper	526-7		x
Exp. of Lab/Sports & Functions	528-9		x
Withholding Tax/Bank Charges	533-4		x
Others			x
Compulsory Contrib.(Deduction)	502	x	
Cash/Bank	100/105	x	
Total			

Prepared By   Approved By

Step 03: Classifying the Financial Activity/Transaction

After one or more transactions are recorded in the journal or voucher, then the next step is to classify them. In this step, we separate each recorded entry and transfer their respective amounts under each respective head of accounts for example amounts recorded against tuition fee should be transferred to tuition fee head (Ledger) and amount recorded against cash should be transferred to Cash Ledger/book.

In simple words, we can say that we just post each entry made in the respective journals/vouchers into their respective ledgers. This process is also called posting. The important thing to remember is that the debit balances should be posted under debit balance in the respective ledger and vice versa.

For example

Cash Received against tuition fee is recorded and posted as follows:

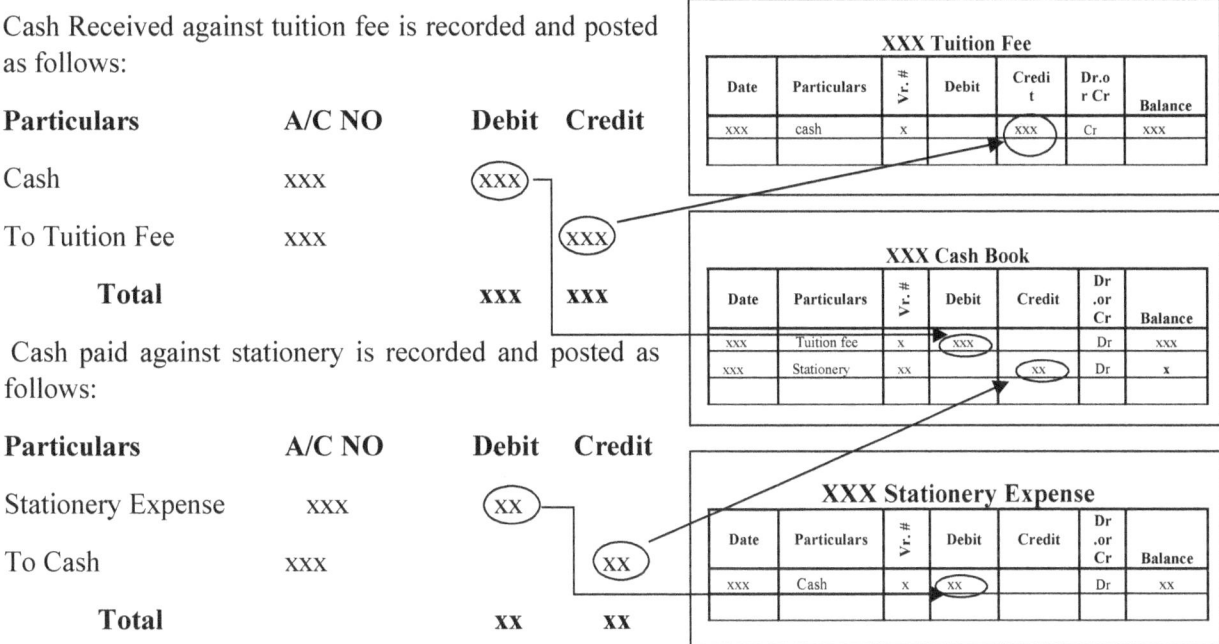

Particulars	A/C NO	Debit	Credit
Cash	xxx	XXX	
To Tuition Fee	xxx		XXX
Total		**xxx**	**xxx**

Cash paid against stationery is recorded and posted as follows:

Particulars	A/C NO	Debit	Credit
Stationery Expense	xxx	XX	
To Cash	xxx		XX
Total		**xx**	**xx**

In the above two examples, amount of tuition fee is as it is posted or transferred to the credit column of the Tuition Fee Ledger and tuition fee ledger has credit balance on xxx date. Other effect of cash account is that the debit balance amount of cash is transferred to the debit side of the cash ledger and credit amount of cash in the second entry is posted in the credit column of the cash ledger. Since Debit balance is more than the Credit Balance to Cash ledger balance Debit Balance (Debit Amount minus Credit Amount = Debit or Credit Balance). Debit column amount of Stationery Expense is as it is posted in the debit column of the Stationery Expense Ledger.

Step 04: Summarizing the Financial Activity/Transaction

Once we have completed first three steps of the booking keeping, we are now in a position to summarize the book keeping process after completing this step. This step is considered the easiest and simplest step of all because in this step we just need to put the **total debit and credit balances** of the ledger accounts into trial balance.

6

For example

After posting the transactions in the Cash Ledger/Book, Tuition fee and Stationery expenses, the next step is to transfer their monthly totals into April Trial Balance. Since there wasn't any other transaction in the tuition fee column so we make totals of all three ledgers and transfer their total monthly balances in the trial balance. Total Credit balance of Tuition Fee ledger is transferred to the credit column of the current month in the trial balance. Similarly, total monthly debit balance of the stationery expenses ledger is transferred to the debit column of the current month of the trial balance. Cash ledger both debit and credit balances are transferred to the trial balance in the respective columns of the current month of the April trial balance.

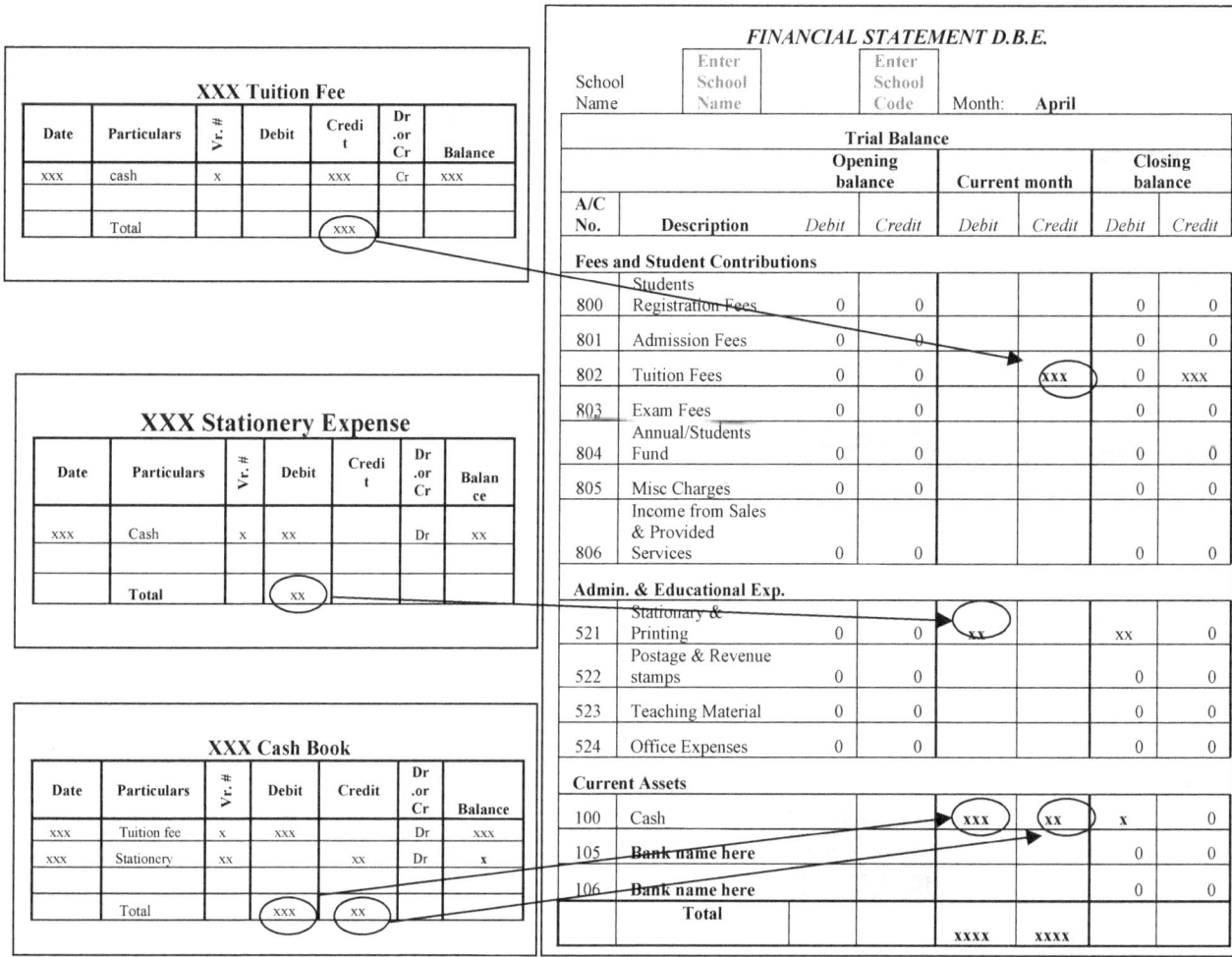

Once all the debit and credit balances of the ledgers are being transferred to the trial balance and the trial balance debit total side is equal to the trial balance total credit side, then only we have completed this book keeping process. We can add some reconciliation checks in order to examine the accuracy of our work.

Part II
Practical Application of Book Keeping

Chapter Two – Practical Exercises of Book Keeping

In the previous chapter, we have tried to understand the book keeping process through four basic steps but now we will use some practical exercises to get better understanding of all these four book keeping steps because book keeping is something which is understood by practice and not by learning only. The more you practice, the better you understand.

Before starting the practical assignments or exercises, we should have some information about the different assignments\exercises and how these are being used and how to practice them.

There are total four exercises 1st and 3rd exercise are related with the receipts i.e., Receipts in the form of Cash in Hand and Cash at Bank and other remaining two exercises (2nd and 4th) are related with the payments through cash and bank. We are recommended that we should get help from the 1st and 2nd exercise and try to solely complete remaining two exercises i.e., 3rd and 4th exercise by ourselves. Once we have completed 3rd and 4th exercise, we should check our work with the solved examples in this book. By following this approach, we will learn more.

Exercise No.1

Receipts during the first half of April 2016

Date	Detail	Amount	Daily Total Amount
1-Apr	Student Registration Fees	500	
	Sale of Forms	500	
	Admission Fee	500	
	Tuition Fee	1,000	
	Annual Fund	800	
	Misc. Charges	200	**3,500**
4-Apr	Tuition Fee	2,500	
	Annual Fund	800	
	Misc. Charges	200	**3,500**
5-Apr	Canteen Income		2,000
6-Apr	Tuition Fee	500	
	Annual Fund	400	
	Misc. Charges	100	**1,000**
7-Apr	Tuition Fee	500	
	Annual Fund	400	
	Misc. Charges	100	**1,000**
8-Apr	Tuition Fee	1,000	
	Annual Fund	800	
	Misc. Charges	200	**2,000**
11-Apr	Grant from DBE (Cheque)		10,000
11-Apr	Tuition Fee	500	
	Annual Fund	400	

Date	Detail	Amount	Daily Total Amount
	Misc. Charges	100	**1,000**
12-Apr	Admission Fee	500	
	Tuition Fee	500	
	Annual Fund	400	
	Misc. Charges	100	**1,500**
13-Apr	Sale of Generator (Cheque)		1,000
14-Apr	Tuition Fee	500	
	Annual Fund	400	
	Misc. Charges	100	**1,000**
15-Apr	Admission Fee	500	
	Tuition Fee	500	
	Annual Fund	400	
	Misc. Charges	100	**1,500**
15-Apr	Interest on Investment		5,000
15-Apr	Cash withdrawn from Bank		20,000

Exercise No.2

Payments during the first half of April 2016

Date	Detail	Amount	Daily Total Amount
1-Apr	Stationery Purchased	1,000	
1-Apr	Refreshment (Tea, Milk etc.)	2,000	
1-Apr	Cleaning Material	1,000	
1-Apr	Printing Expenses	1,000	
1-Apr	Overtime Payment for March 2016	1,500	**6,500**
4-Apr	Books for School Teachers		1,000
5-Apr	EOBI Payment for March 2016		2,600
6-Apr	Bank Statement Charges (Bank)		50
7-Apr	Water Pump Repairing Charges		2,000
8-Apr	Electricity Bill Payment		3,000
11-Apr	Transportation Charges		500
12-Apr	Postage Expenses		100
13-Apr	News Paper		400
14-Apr	Telephone and Internet Expenses		1,500
15-Apr	Withholding Tax on Profit(Bank)		500

Exercise No.3

Receipts during the second half of April 2016

Date	Detail	Amount	Daily Total Amount
18-Apr	Fine from Students	300	
18-Apr	Tuition Fee	500	
	Annual Fund	400	
	Misc. Charges	100	**1,300**
19-Apr	Admission Fee	500	
	Tuition Fee	500	
	Annual Fund	400	
	Misc. Charges	100	**1,500**
20-Apr	Tuition Fee	1,000	
	Annual Fund	400	
	Misc. Charges	100	**1,500**
21-Apr	Sale of Diaries	1,000	
21-Apr	Tuition Fee	1,500	
	Annual Fund	400	
	Misc. Charges	100	**3,000**
22-Apr	Tuition Fee	1,000	
	Annual Fund	800	
	Misc. Charges	200	**2,000**
25-Apr	Tuition Fee	500	
	Annual Fund	400	
	Misc. Charges	100	**1,000**
26-Apr	Tuition Fee	500	
	Annual Fund	400	
	Misc. Charges	100	**1,000**
27-Apr	Grant from Govt. (Cheque)		20,000
28-Apr	Tuition Fee	500	
	Annual Fund	400	
	Misc. Charges	100	**1,000**
29-Apr	Admission Fee	1,000	
	Tuition Fee	1,500	
	Annual Fund	1200	
	Misc. Charges	300	**4,000**
29-Apr	Cash Withdrawn from Bank for Salaries		50,000
30-Apr	Interest on Saving Account		600

Exercise No.4

Payments during the second half of April 2016

Date	Detail	Amount	Daily Total Amount
18-Apr	Stationery for Teachers and Office		1,000
19-Apr	Refreshment Expenses		3,000
20-Apr	Gas Bill		1,000
21-Apr	New Water Pump purchased		10,000
22-Apr	Class Room Repairing work		2,000
25-Apr	New Computer System for Office		10,000
26-Apr	Transportation		1,000
27-Apr	Furniture Repairing Charges		1,500
28-Apr	Salaries Paid to Teaching Staff		46,935
28-Apr	Salaries Paid to Non Teaching Staff		9,095
29-Apr	Provident Fund Payment to CPF		4,500
30-Apr	Withholding tax on Interest		60

Chapter Three – Step 1 Analyzing the Financial Activity

Exercise 1

In the first exercise, the following documents are being used as source documents against respective financial activities or transactions:

April 01, 2016

For Students Registration Fees and Sales of Forms the following income form can be used as a source document. It is recommended to issue receipt from fee receipt book under other income head instead of income form.

Income Form		**Income Form**	
	No.		No.
Date: April 01, 2016		Date: April 01, 2016	
Amount: Rs. 500		Amount: Rs. 500	
Cash/Ch. **Cash**		Cash/Ch. **Cash**	
From: **XYZ**		From: **XYZ**	
School/unit:		School/unit:	
Against /Purpose:		Against /Purpose:	
Students' Registration Fee		Sale of admission forms	
Approved: ___ Received: ___		Approved: ___ Received: ___	

For tuition fee, Carbon copies of the fee receipts and daily summery after getting checked and approved from the approving authority.

Date	1-Apr	Receipt No	1111
Student	Asher	Class	2

Admission Fee	-	
Tuition Fee	500	For April Only
Annual\Student Fund	400	
Extra Charges	100	
Total	**1,000**	

Date	1-Apr	Receipt No	1112
Student	Zain	Class	Nursery

Admission Fee	500	
Tuition Fee	500	For April Only
Annual\Student Fund	400	
Extra Charges	100	
Total	**1,500**	

Daily Fee Summary

Date	Receipt No.	Admission Fee	Tuition Fee	Annual /Student Fund	Extra Student Charges
April 01	1111	-	500	400	100
	1112	500	500	400	100
	Total	**500**	**1,000**	**800**	**200**

Source Documents for Tuition Fee from April 04, 2016 – April 05, 2016

Date	4-Apr		**Receipt No**	1113
Student	Ismail		**Class**	3
Admission Fee	0	For March, April		
Tuition Fee	1,000			
Annual\Student Fund	400			
Extra Charges	100			
Total	**1,500**			

Date	4-Apr		**Receipt No**	1114
Student	Shakeel		**Class**	2
Admission Fee	0			
Tuition Fee	1,500	For Mar., April and May		
Annual\Student Fund	400			
Extra Charges	100			
Total	**2,000**			

Date	6-Apr		**Receipt No**	1115
Student	Zurbabul		**Class**	1
Admission Fee	0			
Tuition Fee	500	For April Only		
Annual\Student Fund	400			
Extra Charges	100			
Total	**1,000**			

Date	7-Apr		**Receipt No**	1116
Student	Naeem		**Class**	1
Admission Fee	0			
Tuition Fee	500	For April Only		
Annual\Student Fund	400			
Extra Charges	100			
Total	**1,000**			

Date	8-Apr		**Receipt No**	1117
Student	Kashif		**Class**	2
Admission Fee	0			
Tuition Fee	500	For April Only		
Annual\Student Fund	400			
Extra Charges	100			
Total	**1,000**			

Date	8-Apr		**Receipt No**	1118
Student	Mohsin		**Class**	3
Admission Fee	0			
Tuition Fee	500	For April Only		
Annual\Student Fund	400			
Extra Charges	100			
Total	**1,000**			

Date	11-Apr		**Receipt No**	1119
Student	Shan		**Class**	1
Admission Fee	0			
Tuition Fee	500	For April Only		
Annual\Student Fund	400			
Extra Charges	100			
Total	**1,000**			

Date	12-Apr		**Receipt No**	1120
Student	Nathaniel		**Class**	Nursery
Admission Fee	500			
Tuition Fee	500	For April Only		
Annual\Student Fund	400			
Extra Charges	100			
Total	**1,500**			

Date	14-Apr		Receipt No	1121
Student	Sohail		**Class**	3
	Admission Fee	0		
	Tuition Fee	500	For April Only	
	Annual\Student Fund	400		
	Extra Charges	100		
	Total	**1,000**		

Date	15-Apr		Receipt No	1122
Student	Adnan		**Class**	Nursery
	Admission Fee	500		
	Tuition Fee	500	For April Only	
	Annual\Student Fund	400		
	Extra Charges	100		
	Total	**1,500**		

Daily Fee Summary

Date	Receipt No.	Admission Fee	Tuition Fee	Annual /Student Fund	Extra Student Charges
April 01	1111	-	500	400	100
	1112	500	500	400	100
	Total	**500**	**1,000**	**800**	**200**
Apr 04	1113	-	1,000	400	100
	1114	-	1,500	400	100
	Total	**-**	**2,500**	**800**	**200**
Apr 06	1115	-	500	400	100
	Total	**-**	**500**	**400**	**100**
Apr 07	1116	-	500	400	100
	Total	**-**	**500**	**400**	**100**
Apr 08	1117	-	500	400	100
	1118	-	500	400	100
	Total	**-**	**1,000**	**800**	**200**
Apr 11	1119	-	500	400	100
	Total	**-**	**500**	**400**	**100**
Apr 12	1120	500	500	400	100
	Total	**500**	**500**	**400**	**100**
Apr 14	1121	-	500	400	100
	Total	**-**	**500**	**400**	**100**
Apr 15	1122	500	500	400	100
	Total	**500**	**500**	**400**	**100**

From April 04, 2016 till April 15, 2016 Income other than tuition fee

Income Form
No.

Date: April 04, 2016

Amount: Rs. 2,000

Cash/Ch. Cash

From: XYZ

School/unit: _____

Against /Purpose: _____

Canteen Rent

Approved: ___ Received: ___

Income Form
No.

Date: April 11, 2016

Amount: Rs. 10,000

Cash/Ch. abc

From: XYZ

School/unit: _____

Against /Purpose: _____

Grant from DBE

Approved: ___ Received: ___

<table>
<tr><td colspan="2">

Income Form

No.

Date: April 13, 2016

Amount: Rs. 1,000

Cash/Ch. Abc

From: XYZ

School/unit: _____

Against /Purpose:

Sale of Generator

_____

_____

_____

Approved: ___   Received: ___

</td><td colspan="2">

Income Form

No.

Date: April 15, 2016

Amount: Rs. 5,000

Cash/Ch. Bank Transfer

From: XYZ

School/unit: _____

Against /Purpose:

Interest on Investment

_____

_____

_____

Approved: ___   Received: ___

</td></tr>
</table>

Note: For Cash withdrawal photocopy of the signed cheque can be used as a supporting source document.

Exercise 2

Supporting source document for payment transactions are used as follows from April 01 – 15, 2016.

EXPENSE FORM								
Name:		School/unit:				Date:	1-Apr	
Date	Description	Stationary/Print	Office expenses	Telephone	Petrol /Transport	Other	Total	Acc. No.
1-Apr	Stationery Purchased	1000					1000	521
1-Apr	Refreshment (Tea, Milk etc.)		2000				2000	524
1-Apr	Cleaning Material		1000				1000	524
1-Apr	Printing Expenses	1000					1000	521
1-Apr	Overtime Payment for March 2016					1500	1500	504
Total		**2,000**	**3,000**	**-**	**-**	**1,500**	**6,500**	

Receipts have to be attached

Checked by: Approved by: Received by:

16

Expense form A

Date:	4-Apr		No.
Amount:	1000	Cheque No.	
To:		Acc. No:	523
School/unit:			
Purpose:	Books for School Teachers		

Approved by: _____ Received by: _____

Expense form A

Date:	5-Apr		No.
Amount:	2600	Cheque No.	
To:		Acc. No:	502
School/unit:			
Purpose:	EOBI Payment		

Approved by: _____ Received by: _____

Expense form A

Date:	6-Apr		No.
Amount:	50	Cheque No.	
To:		Acc. No:	534
School/unit:			
Purpose:	Bank Charges		

Approved by: _____ Received by: _____

Expense form A

Date:	7-Apr		No.
Amount:	2000	Cheque No.	
To:		Acc. No:	518
School/unit:			
Purpose:	Water Pump Repairing Work		

Approved by: _____ Received by: _____

Expense form A

Date:	8-Apr		No.
Amount:	3000	Cheque No.	
To:		Acc. No:	506
School/unit:			
Purpose:	Electricity Bill Paid		

Approved by: _____ Received by: _____

Expense form A

Date:	11-Apr		No.
Amount:	500	Cheque No.	
To:		Acc. No:	525
School/unit:			
Purpose:	Transportation		

Approved by: _____ Received by: _____

	Expense form A				Expense form A		
Date:	12-Apr		No.	Date:	13-Apr		No.
Amount:	100	Cheque No.		Amount:	400	Cheque No.	
To:		Acc. No:	522	To:		Acc. No:	527
School/unit:				School/unit:			
Purpose:	Postage Expenses			Purpose:	Monthly News Papers Bills Paid		
Approved by:		Received by:		Approved by:		Received by:	

	Expense form A				Expense form A		
Date:	14-Apr		No.	Date:	15-Apr		No.
Amount:	1500	Cheque No.		Amount:	500	Cheque No.	
To:		Acc. No:	509	To:		Acc. No:	533
School/unit:				School/unit:			
Purpose:	Telephone and Internet Expenses			Purpose:	Withholding Tax on Interest		
Approved by:		Received by:		Approved by:		Received by:	

Note: For Cash withdrawal photocopy of the signed cheque can be used as a supporting source document.

Exercise 3

Supporting source document for Tuition Fee Receipts are used as follows from April 16 – 30, 2016.

Date	18-Apr		**Receipt No**	1123
Student	Manasseh		**Class**	2
	Admission Fee	-	For April Only	
	Tuition Fee	500		
	Annual\Student Fund	400		
	Extra Charges	100		
	Total	**1,000**		

Date	19-Apr		**Receipt No**	1124
Student	Jesse		**Class**	Nursery
	Admission Fee	500	For April Only	
	Tuition Fee	500		
	Annual\Student Fund	400		
	Extra Charges	100		
	Total	**1,500**		

Date	20-Apr		Receipt No	1125
Student	Fayyaz		Class	3

Admission Fee	0	
Tuition Fee	1,000	For April, May
Annual\Student Fund	400	
Extra Charges	100	
Total	**1,500**	

Date	21-Apr		Receipt No	1126
Student	Khurram		Class	2

Admission Fee	0	
Tuition Fee	1,500	For April, May and June
Annual\Student Fund	400	
Extra Charges	100	
Total	**2,000**	

Date	22-Apr		Receipt No	1127
Student	Waqar		Class	1

Admission Fee	0	
Tuition Fee	500	For April Only
Annual\Student Fund	400	
Extra Charges	100	
Total	**1,000**	

Date	22-Apr		Receipt No	1128
Student	Haroon		Class	1

Admission Fee	0	
Tuition Fee	500	For April Only
Annual\Student Fund	400	
Extra Charges	100	
Total	**1,000**	

Date	25-Apr		Receipt No	1129
Student	Ahsan		Class	2

Admission Fee	0	
Tuition Fee	500	For April Only
Annual\Student Fund	400	
Extra Charges	100	
Total	**1,000**	

Date	26-Apr		Receipt No	1130
Student	Simon		Class	3

Admission Fee	0	
Tuition Fee	500	For April Only
Annual\Student Fund	400	
Extra Charges	100	
Total	**1,000**	

Date	28-Apr		Receipt No	1131
Student	Bilal		Class	1

Admission Fee	0	
Tuition Fee	500	For April Only
Annual\Student Fund	400	
Extra Charges	100	
Total	**1,000**	

Date	29-Apr		Receipt No	1132
Student	Zeeshan		Class	Nursery

Admission Fee	500	
Tuition Fee	500	For April Only
Annual\Student Fund	400	
Extra Charges	100	
Total	**1,500**	

Date	29-Apr		Receipt No	1133
Student	Anwar		Class	3

Admission Fee	0	
Tuition Fee	500	For April Only
Annual\Student Fund	400	
Extra Charges	100	
Total	**1,000**	

Date	29-Apr		Receipt No	1134
Student	Zubair		Class	Nursery

Admission Fee	500	
Tuition Fee	500	For April Only
Annual\Student Fund	400	
Extra Charges	100	
Total	**1,500**	

Daily Fee Summary

Date	Receipt No.	Admission Fee	Tuition Fee	Annual /Student Fund	Extra Student Charges
April 01	1111	-	500	400	100
	1112	500	500	400	100
	Total	500	1,000	800	200
Apr 04	1113	-	1,000	400	100
	1114	-	1,500	400	100
	Total	-	2,500	800	200
Apr 06	1115	-	500	400	100
	Total	-	500	400	100
Apr 07	1116	-	500	400	100
	Total	-	500	400	100
Apr 08	1117	-	500	400	100
	1118	-	500	400	100
	Total	-	1,000	800	200
Apr 11	1119	-	500	400	100
	Total	-	500	400	100
Apr 12	1120	500	500	400	100
	Total	500	500	400	100
Apr 14	1121	-	500	400	100
	Total	-	500	400	100
Apr 15	1122	500	500	400	100
	Total	500	500	400	100

Daily Fee Summary

Date	Receipt No.	Admission Fee	Tuition Fee	Annual /Student Fund	Extra Student Charges
April 18	1123	-	500	400	100
	Total	-	500	400	100
Apr 19	1124	500	500	400	100
	Total	500	500	400	100
Apr 20	1125	0	1,000	400	100
	Total	0	1,000	400	100
Apr 21	1126	0	1,500	400	100
	Total	0	1,500	400	100
Apr 22	1127	0	500	400	100
	1128	0	500	400	100
	Total	0	1,000	800	200
Apr 25	1129	0	500	400	100
	Total	0	500	400	100
Apr 26	1130	0	500	400	100
	Total	0	500	400	100
Apr 28	1131	0	500	400	100
	Total	0	500	400	100
Apr 29	1132	500	500	400	100
	1133	0	500	400	100
	1134	500	500	400	100
	Total	1,000	1,500	1,200	300
Monthly Total		3,000	15,000	9,600	2,400

Supporting source document for other than Tuition Fee Receipts are used as follows from April 16 – 30, 2016.

Income Form

No. ____

Date: April 18, 2016

Amount: Rs. 300

Cash/Ch. Cash

From: XYZ

School/unit: _____

Against /Purpose: _____

Fine from Students

Approved: ____   Received: ____

Income Form

No. ____

Date: April 21, 2016

Amount: Rs. 1,000

Cash/Ch. Cash

From: XYZ

School/unit: _____

Against /Purpose: _____

Sale of Diaries

Approved: ____   Received: ____

<table>
<tr><td colspan="2" align="center">Income Form</td></tr>
<tr><td></td><td align="right">No.</td></tr>
<tr><td>Date:</td><td>April 27, 2016</td></tr>
<tr><td>Amount:</td><td>Rs. 20,000</td></tr>
<tr><td>Cash/Ch.</td><td>abc</td></tr>
<tr><td>From:</td><td>XYZ</td></tr>
<tr><td>School/unit:</td><td></td></tr>
<tr><td>Against /Purpose:</td><td></td></tr>
<tr><td colspan="2">Grant from Government</td></tr>
<tr><td>Approved: ___</td><td>Received: ___</td></tr>
</table>

<table>
<tr><td colspan="2" align="center">Income Form</td></tr>
<tr><td></td><td align="right">No.</td></tr>
<tr><td>Date:</td><td>April 18, 2016</td></tr>
<tr><td>Amount:</td><td>Rs. 600</td></tr>
<tr><td>Cash/Ch.</td><td>Bank Transfer</td></tr>
<tr><td>From:</td><td>XYZ</td></tr>
<tr><td>School/unit:</td><td></td></tr>
<tr><td>Against /Purpose:</td><td></td></tr>
<tr><td colspan="2">Interest on Saving Bank Account</td></tr>
<tr><td>Approved: ___</td><td>Received: ___</td></tr>
</table>

Note: For Cash withdrawal photocopy of the signed cheque can be used as a supporting source document.

Exercise 4

Supporting source document for payment transactions are used as follows from April 16 – 30, 2016.

Expense form A

No.

Date: 18-Apr
Amount: 1000   Cheque No. ____
To: Acc. No: 521
School/unit:
Purpose: Stationery Purchased

Approved by: ___   Received by: _____

Expense form A

No.

Date: 19-Apr
Amount: 3000   Cheque No. ____
To: Acc. No: 524
School/unit:
Purpose: Refreshment Expenses   Refreshment Expenses

Approved by: ___   Received by: _____

Expense form A

No.

Date: 20-Apr
Amount: 1000   Cheque No. ____
To: Acc. No: 508
School/unit:
Purpose: Gas Bill Paid

Approved by: ___   Received by: _____

Expense form A

No.

Date: 21-Apr
Amount: 10000   Cheque No. ____
To: Acc. No: 514
School/unit:
Purpose: New Water Pump Purchased

Approved by: ___   Received by: _____

Expense form A

No. _____

Date: 22-Apr

Amount: _____ 2000   Cheque No. _____

To: _____ Acc. No: __517__

School/unit: _____

Purpose: Class Room Repairing Work _____

_____

_____

Approved by: ___   Received by: _____

Expense form A

No. _____

Date: 25-Apr

Amount: _____ 10000   Cheque No. _____

To: _____ Acc. No: __515__

School/unit: _____

Purpose: New Computer System Purchased _____

_____

_____

Approved by: ___   Received by: _____

Expense form A

No. _____

Date: 26-Apr

Amount: _____ 1000   Cheque No. _____

To: _____ Acc. No: __525__

School/unit: _____

Purpose: Transportation Expenses Paid _____

_____

_____

Approved by: ___   Received by: _____

Expense form A

No. _____

Date: 27-Apr

Amount: _____ 1500   Cheque No. _____

To: _____ Acc. No: __518__

School/unit: _____

Purpose: Furniture Repairing Charges _____

_____

_____

Approved by: ___   Received by: _____

Expense form A

No. _____

Date: 29-Apr

Amount: _____ 4500   Cheque No. _____

To: _____ Acc. No: __502__

School/unit: _____

Purpose: Provident Fund Payment _____

_____

_____

Approved by: ___   Received by: _____

Expense form A

No. _____

Date: 30-Apr

Amount: _____ 60   Cheque No. _____

To: _____ Acc. No: __533__

School/unit: _____

Purpose: Withholding Tax Deducted _____

_____

_____

Approved by: ___   Received by: _____

For Salaries Salary Register/Pay slips/Salary Statement can be used as source document which is as follows:

Name of the School

Salary Statement/Register for the Month of April 2016

S.No.	Name	Scale	Basic	House Rent	Utility All.	Other	Gross	E.O.B.I	Provident Fund	Deductions	Net Pay	Signature
Teaching Staff												
1	A	xx.xx	12,000	4,800	2,400	1,200	20,400	130	750	-	19,520	
2	B	xx.xx	9,000	3,600	1,800	-	14,400	130	563	-	13,708	
3	C	xx.xx	9,000	3,600	1,800	-	14,400	130	563	-	13,708	
Sub-Total			30,000	12,000	6,000	1,200	49,200	390	1,875	-	46,935	
Non Teaching												
4	Z	xx.xx	6,000	2,400	1,200	-	9,600	130	375	-	9,095	
Sub-Total			6,000	2,400	1,200	-	9,600	130	375	-	9,095	
Total			36,000	14,400	7,200	1,200	58,800	520	2,250	-	56,030	

	Empoyee	Employer	Total
EOBI	520	2,080	2,600
Provident Fund	2,250	2,250	4,500

_____Prepare By_____   _____Approved By_____

Chapter Four – Step 2 Recording the Financial Activity

In the previous chapter, with the help of the source document we have been able to analyze the financial activity, now we are moving to the next step where we will record all the financial activities from exercise 1 – 4 and attached each relevant source document with the respective financial activity and get it approved from the relevant authority.

Exercise 1

The following receipt vouchers will be prepared against each financial activity perform from April 01 – 15, 2016 in this exercise.

Receipt Voucher (Cash\Bank)

Date : April 05, 2016
Payee :
Voucher No 1003
Rupees: 2,000/-
Cheque No.

Particulars	A\C No.	Debit	Credit
Cash	100	2000	x
Bank	105		x
To Student Registration Fee	800	x	
To Admission Fees	801	x	
To Tuition Fees	802	x	
To Exam Fees	803	x	
To Annual/Student Fund	804	x	
To Misc. Charges	805	x	
To Income from Sales	806	x	2000
To Interest On Saving	807	x	
To Interest on Investment	808	x	
To Grants/Donations Congre	809	x	
To Grants/Donations DBE	810	x	
To Diocese Contribution	811	x	
To Other Donations	812	x	
To Income from Org. Activities	813	x	
To Other Income	814	x	
To Others	815	x	
		x	
		x	
		x	
Total		2000	2000

Prepared By   Approved By

Receipt Voucher (Cash\Bank)

Date : April 04, 2016
Payee :
Voucher No 1002
Rupees: 3,500/-
Cheque No.

Particulars	A\C No.	Debit	Credit
Cash	100	3500	x
Bank	105	0	x
To Student Registration Fee	800	x	
To Admission Fees	801	x	
To Tuition Fees	802	x	2500
To Exam Fees	803	x	0
To Annual/Student Fund	804	x	800
To Misc. Charges	805	x	200
To Income from Sales	806	x	
To Interest On Saving	807	x	
To Interest on Investment	808	x	
To Grants/Donations Congre	809	x	
To Grants/Donations DBE	810	x	
To Diocese Contribution	811	x	
To Other Donations	812	x	
To Income from Org. Activities	813	x	
To Other Income	814	x	
To Others	815	x	
		x	
		x	
		x	
Total		3500	3500

Prepared By   Approved By

Receipt Voucher (Cash\Bank)

Date : April 01, 2016
Payee :
Voucher No 1001
Rupees: 3,500/-
Cheque No.

Particulars	A\C No.	Debit	Credit
Cash	100	3500	x
Bank	105		x
To Student Registration Fee	800	x	500
To Admission Fees	801	x	500
To Tuition Fees	802	x	1000
To Exam Fees	803	x	0
To Annual/Student Fund	804	x	800
To Misc. Charges	805	x	700
To Income from Sales	806	x	
To Interest On Saving	807	x	
To Interest on Investment	808	x	
To Grants/Donations Congre	809	x	
To Grants/Donations DBE	810	x	
To Diocese Contribution	811	x	
To Other Donations	812	x	
To Income from Org. Activities	813	x	
To Other Income	814	x	
To Others	815	x	
		x	
		x	
		x	
Total		3500	3500

Prepared By   Approved By

Receipt Voucher (Cash\Bank)

Date : April 08, 2016

Payee : _____ Voucher No 1006
Rupees: 2,000/- Cheque No.

Particulars	A\C No.	Debit	Credit
Cash	100	2000	x
Bank	105		x
To Student Registration Fee	800	x	
To Admission Fees	801	x	
To Tuition Fees	802	x	1000
To Exam Fees	803	x	
To Annual/Student Fund	804	x	800
To Misc. Charges	805	x	200
To Income from Sales	806	x	
To Interest On Saving	807	x	
To Interest on Investment	808	x	
To Grants/Donations Congre	809	x	
To Grants/Donations DBE	810	x	
To Diocese Contribution	811	x	
To Other Donations	812	x	
To Income from Org. Activities	813	x	
To Other Income	814	x	
To Others	815	x	
		x	
		x	
		x	
Total		**2000**	**2000**

Prepared By   Approved By

Receipt Voucher (Cash\Bank)

Date : April 07, 2016

Payee : _____ Voucher No 1005
Rupees: 1,000/- Cheque No.

Particulars	A\C No.	Debit	Credit
Cash	100	1000	x
Bank	105		x
To Student Registration Fee	800	x	
To Admission Fees	801	x	
To Tuition Fees	802	x	500
To Exam Fees	803	x	
To Annual/Student Fund	804	x	400
To Misc. Charges	805	x	100
To Income from Sales	806	x	
To Interest On Saving	807	x	
To Interest on Investment	808	x	
To Grants/Donations Congre	809	x	
To Grants/Donations DBE	810	x	
To Diocese Contribution	811	x	
To Other Donations	812	x	
To Income from Org. Activities	813	x	
To Other Income	814	x	
To Others	815	x	
		x	
		x	
		x	
Total		**1000**	**1000**

Prepared By   Approved By

Receipt Voucher (Cash\Bank)

Date : April 06, 2016

Payee : _____ Voucher No 1004
Rupees: 1,000/- Cheque No.

Particulars	A\C No.	Debit	Credit
Cash	100	1000	x
Bank	105		x
To Student Registration Fee	800	x	
To Admission Fees	801	x	
To Tuition Fees	802	x	500
To Exam Fees	803	x	0
To Annual/Student Fund	804	x	400
To Misc. Charges	805	x	100
To Income from Sales	806	x	
To Interest On Saving	807	x	
To Interest on Investment	808	x	
To Grants/Donations Congre	809	x	
To Grants/Donations DBE	810	x	
To Diocese Contribution	811	x	
To Other Donations	812	x	
To Income from Org. Activities	813	x	
To Other Income	814	x	
To Others	815	x	
		x	
		x	
		x	
Total		**1000**	**1000**

Prepared By   Approved By

Receipt Voucher (Cash\Bank)

Date : April 12, 2016

Payee : _____ Voucher No 1009
Rupees: 1,500/- Cheque No.

Particulars	A\C No.	Debit	Credit
Cash	100	1500	x
Bank	105		x
To Student Registration Fee	800	x	
To Admission Fees	801	x	500
To Tuition Fees	802	x	500
To Exam Fees	803	x	
To Annual/Student Fund	804	x	400
To Misc. Charges	805	x	100
To Income from Sales	806	x	
To Interest On Saving	807	x	
To Interest on Investment	808	x	
To Grants/Donations Congre	809	x	
To Grants/Donations DBE	810	x	
To Diocese Contribution	811	x	
To Other Donations	812	x	
To Income from Org. Activities	813	x	
To Other Income	814	x	
To Others	815	x	
		x	
		x	
		x	
Total		**1500**	**1500**

Prepared By   Approved By

Receipt Voucher (Cash\Bank)

Date : April 11, 2016

Payee : _____ Voucher No 1008
Rupees: 1,000/- Cheque No.

Particulars	A\C No.	Debit	Credit
Cash	100	1000	x
Bank	105		x
To Student Registration Fee	800	x	
To Admission Fees	801	x	
To Tuition Fees	802	x	500
To Exam Fees	803	x	
To Annual/Student Fund	804	x	400
To Misc. Charges	805	x	100
To Income from Sales	806	x	
To Interest On Saving	807	x	
To Interest on Investment	808	x	
To Grants/Donations Congre	809	x	
To Grants/Donations DBE	810	x	
To Diocesc Contribution	811	x	
To Other Donations	812	x	
To Income from Org. Activities	813	x	
To Other Income	814	x	
To Others	815	x	
		x	
		x	
		x	
Total		**1000**	**1000**

Prepared By   Approved By

Receipt Voucher (Cash\Bank)

Date : April 11, 2016

Payee : _____ Voucher No 1007
Rupees: 10,000/- Cheque No.

Particulars	A\C No.	Debit	Credit
Cash	100		x
Bank	105	10000	x
To Student Registration Fee	800	x	
To Admission Fees	801	x	
To Tuition Fees	802	x	
To Exam Fees	803	x	
To Annual/Student Fund	804	x	
To Misc. Charges	805	x	
To Income from Sales	806	x	
To Interest On Saving	807	x	
To Interest on Investment	808	x	
To Grants/Donations Congre	809	x	
To Grants/Donations DBE	810	x	10000
To Diocese Contribution	811	x	
To Other Donations	812	x	
To Income from Org. Activities	813	x	
To Other Income	814	x	
To Others	815	x	
		x	
		x	
		x	
Total		**10000**	**10000**

Prepared By   Approved By

Receipt Voucher (Cash\Bank)

Date : _____
Payee : _____   Voucher No: 1012
Rupees: _____   Cheque No.

Particulars	A\C No.	Debit	Credit
Cash	100		x
Bank	105		x
To Student Registration Fee	800	x	
To Admission Fees	801	x	
To Tuition Fees	802	x	
To Exam Fees	803	x	
To Annual/Student Fund	804	x	
To Misc. Charges	805	x	
To Income from Sales	806	x	
To Interest On Saving	807	x	
To Interest on Investment	808	x	
To Grants/Donations Congre	809	x	
To Grants/Donations DBE	810	x	
To Diocese Contribution	811	x	
To Other Donations	812	x	
To Income from Org. Activities	813	x	
To Other Income	814	x	
To Others	815	x	
		x	
		x	
		x	
Total		**0**	**0**

Prepared By   Approved By

Receipt Voucher (Cash\Bank)

Date : April 14, 2016
Payee : _____   Voucher No: 1011
Rupees: 1,000/-   Cheque No.

Particulars	A\C No.	Debit	Credit
Cash	100	1000	x
Bank	105		x
To Student Registration Fee	800	x	
To Admission Fees	801	x	
To Tuition Fees	802	x	500
To Exam Fees	803	x	
To Annual/Student Fund	804	x	400
To Misc. Charges	805	x	100
To Income from Sales	806	x	
To Interest On Saving	807	x	
To Interest on Investment	808	x	
To Grants/Donations Congre	809	x	
To Grants/Donations DBE	810	x	
To Diocese Contribution	811	x	
To Other Donations	812	x	
To Income from Org. Activities	813	x	
To Other Income	814	x	
To Others	815	x	
		x	
		x	
		x	
Total		**1000**	**1000**

Prepared By   Approved By

Receipt Voucher (Cash\Bank)

Date : April 13, 2016
Payee : _____   Voucher No: 1010
Rupees: 1,000/-   Cheque No.

Particulars	A\C No.	Debit	Credit
Cash	100		x
Bank	105	1000	x
To Student Registration Fee	800	x	
To Admission Fees	801	x	
To Tuition Fees	802	x	
To Exam Fees	803	x	
To Annual/Student Fund	804	x	
To Misc. Charges	805	x	
To Income from Sales	806	x	1000
To Interest On Saving	807	x	
To Interest on Investment	808	x	
To Grants/Donations Congre	809	x	
To Grants/Donations DBE	810	x	
To Diocese Contribution	811	x	
To Other Donations	812	x	
To Income from Org. Activities	813	x	
To Other Income	814	x	
To Others	815	x	
		x	
		x	
		x	
Total		**1000**	**1000**

Prepared By   Approved By

Receipt Voucher (Cash\Bank)

Date : April 15, 2016
Payee : _____   Voucher No: 1015
Rupees: 20,000/-   Cheque No.

Particulars	A\C No.	Debit	Credit
Cash	100	20000	x
Bank	105		x
To Student Registration Fee	800	x	
To Admission Fees	801	x	
To Tuition Fees	802	x	
To Exam Fees	803	x	
To Annual/Student Fund	804	x	
To Misc. Charges	805	x	
To Income from Sales	806	x	
To Interest On Saving	807	x	
To Interest on Investment	808	x	
To Grants/Donations Congre	809	x	
To Grants/Donations DBE	810	x	
To Diocese Contribution	811	x	
To Other Donations	812	x	
To Income from Org. Activities	813	x	
To Other Income	814	x	
To Others	815	x	
		x	
To Bank	105	x	20000
		x	
Total		**20000**	**20000**

Prepared By   Approved By

Receipt Voucher (Cash\Bank)

Date : April 15, 2016
Payee : _____   Voucher No: 1014
Rupees: 5,000/-   Cheque No.

Particulars	A\C No.	Debit	Credit
Cash	100		x
Bank	105	5000	x
To Student Registration Fee	800	x	
To Admission Fees	801	x	
To Tuition Fees	802	x	
To Exam Fees	803	x	
To Annual/Student Fund	804	x	
To Misc. Charges	805	x	
To Income from Sales	806	x	
To Interest On Saving	807	x	
To Interest on Investment	808	x	5000
To Grants/Donations Congre	809	x	
To Grants/Donations DBE	810	x	
To Diocese Contribution	811	x	
To Other Donations	812	x	
To Income from Org. Activities	813	x	
To Other Income	814	x	
To Others	815	x	
		x	
		x	
		x	
Total		**5000**	**5000**

Prepared By   Approved By

Receipt Voucher (Cash\Bank)

Date : April 15, 2016
Payee : _____   Voucher No: 1013
Rupees: 1,500/-   Cheque No.

Particulars	A\C No.	Debit	Credit
Cash	100	1500	x
Bank	105		x
To Student Registration Fee	800	x	
To Admission Fees	801	x	500
To Tuition Fees	802	x	500
To Exam Fees	803	x	
To Annual/Student Fund	804	x	400
To Misc. Charges	805	x	100
To Income from Sales	806	x	
To Interest On Saving	807	x	
To Interest on Investment	808	x	
To Grants/Donations Congre	809	x	
To Grants/Donations DBE	810	x	
To Diocese Contribution	811	x	
To Other Donations	812	x	
To Income from Org. Activities	813	x	
To Other Income	814	x	
To Others	815	x	
		x	
		x	
		x	
Total		**1500**	**1500**

Prepared By   Approved By

Exercise 2

The following payment vouchers will be prepared against each financial activity.

Payment Voucher (Cash\Bank)
Date: April 05, 2016
Payee: _____ Voucher No: 2003
Rupees: 2,600/- Cheque No.

Particulars	A\C No.	Debit	Credit
Teachers' Salary	500		x
Other Staff Salaries	501		x
Compulsory Contributions	502	2600	x
Overtime Payment	503		x
Water/Electricity Expenses	506-7		x
Gas/Internet and Telephone	508-9		x
Rent/Insurance/S.S. Charges	510-2		x
Capital Building/Furniture	513-4		x
Capital Equipment/Vehicle	515-16		x
Repairs Building/Furniture	517-8		x
Repairs Equipment/Vehicle	519-20		x
Stationery and Printing Expenses	521		x
Postage and Revenue Expenses	522		x
Teaching Material	523		x
Office Expenses	524		x
Transportation Expenses	525		x
Training /News paper	526-7		x
Expense of Lab/Sports and Functions	528-9		x
Withholding Tax/Bank Charges	533-4		x
Compulsory Contributions(Deductions)	502	x	
Cash/Bank	100/105	x	2600
Total		**2600**	**2600**

Prepared By   Approved By

Payment Voucher (Cash\Bank)
Date: April 04, 2016
Payee: _____ Voucher No: 2002
Rupees: 1,000/- Cheque No.

Particulars	A\C No.	Debit	Credit
Teachers' Salary	500		x
Other Staff Salaries	501		x
Compulsory Contributions	502		x
Overtime Payment	503		x
Water/Electricity Expenses	506-7		x
Gas/Internet and Telephone	508-9		x
Rent/Insurance/S.S. Charges	510-2		x
Capital Building/Furniture	513-4		x
Capital Equipment/Vehicle	515-16		x
Repairs Building/Furniture	517-8		x
Repairs Equipment/Vehicle	519-20		x
Stationery and Printing Expenses	521		x
Postage and Revenue Expenses	522		x
Teaching Material	523	1000	x
Office Expenses	524		x
Transportation Expenses	525		x
Training /News paper	526-7		x
Expense of Lab/Sports and Functions	528-9		x
Withholding Tax/Bank Charges	533-4		x
Compulsory Contributions(Deductions)	502	x	
Cash/Bank	100/105	x	1000
Total		**1000**	**1000**

Prepared By   Approved By

Payment Voucher (Cash\Bank)
Date: April 01, 2016
Payee: _____ Voucher No: 2001
Rupees: 6,500/- Cheque No.

Particulars	A\C No.	Debit	Credit
Teachers' Salary	500		x
Other Staff Salaries	501		x
Compulsory Contributions	502		x
Overtime Payment	503	1500	x
Water/Electricity Expenses	506-7		x
Gas/Internet and Telephone	508-9		x
Rent/Insurance/S.S. Charges	510-2		x
Capital Building/Furniture	513-4		x
Capital Equipment/Vehicle	515-16		x
Repairs Building/Furniture	517-8		x
Repairs Equipment/Vehicle	519-20		x
Stationery and Printing Expenses	521	2000	x
Postage and Revenue Expenses	522		x
Teaching Material	523		x
Office Expenses	524	3000	x
Transportation Expenses	525		x
Training /News paper	526-7		x
Expense of Lab/Sports and Functions	528-9		x
Withholding Tax/Bank Charges	533-4		x
Compulsory Contributions(Deductions)	502	x	
Cash/Bank	100/105	x	6500
Total		**6500**	**6500**

Prepared By   Approved By

Payment Voucher (Cash\Bank)
Date: April 08, 2016
Payee: _____ Voucher No: 2006
Rupees: 3,000/- Cheque No.

Particulars	A\C No.	Debit	Credit
Teachers' Salary	500		x
Other Staff Salaries	501		x
Compulsory Contributions	502		x
Overtime Payment	503		x
Water/Electricity Expenses	506-7	3000	x
Gas/Internet and Telephone	508-9		x
Rent/Insurance/S.S. Charges	510-2		x
Capital Building/Furniture	513-4		x
Capital Equipment/Vehicle	515-16		x
Repairs Building/Furniture	517-8		x
Repairs Equipment/Vehicle	519-20		x
Stationery and Printing Expenses	521		x
Postage and Revenue Expenses	522		x
Teaching Material	523		x
Office Expenses	524		x
Transportation Expenses	525		x
Training /News paper	526-7		x
Expense of Lab/Sports and Functions	528-9		x
Withholding Tax/Bank Charges	533-4		x
Compulsory Contributions(Deductions)	502	x	
Cash/Bank	100/105	x	3000
Total		**3000**	**3000**

Prepared By   Approved By

Payment Voucher (Cash\Bank)
Date: April 07, 2016
Payee: _____ Voucher No: 2005
Rupees: 2,000/- Cheque No.

Particulars	A\C No.	Debit	Credit
Teachers' Salary	500		x
Other Staff Salaries	501		x
Compulsory Contributions	502		x
Overtime Payment	503		x
Water/Electricity Expenses	506-7		x
Gas/Internet and Telephone	508-9		x
Rent/Insurance/S.S. Charges	510-2		x
Capital Building/Furniture	513-4		x
Capital Equipment/Vehicle	515-16		x
Repairs Building/Furniture	517-8	2000	x
Repairs Equipment/Vehicle	519-20		x
Stationery and Printing Expenses	521		x
Postage and Revenue Expenses	522		x
Teaching Material	523		x
Office Expenses	524		x
Transportation Expenses	525		x
Training /News paper	526-7		x
Expense of Lab/Sports and Functions	528-9		x
Withholding Tax/Bank Charges	533-4		x
Compulsory Contributions(Deductions)	502	x	
Cash/Bank	100/105	x	2000
Total		**2000**	**2000**

Prepared By   Approved By

Payment Voucher (Cash\Bank)
Date: April 06, 2016
Payee: _____ Voucher No: 2004
Rupees: 50/- Cheque No.

Particulars	A\C No.	Debit	Credit
Teachers' Salary	500		x
Other Staff Salaries	501		x
Compulsory Contributions	502		x
Overtime Payment	503		x
Water/Electricity Expenses	506-7		x
Gas/Internet and Telephone	508-9		x
Rent/Insurance/S.S. Charges	510-2		x
Capital Building/Furniture	513-4		x
Capital Equipment/Vehicle	515-16		x
Repairs Building/Furniture	517-8		x
Repairs Equipment/Vehicle	519-20		x
Stationery and Printing Expenses	521		x
Postage and Revenue Expenses	522		x
Teaching Material	523		x
Office Expenses	524		x
Transportation Expenses	525		x
Training /News paper	526-7		x
Expense of Lab/Sports and Functions	528-9		x
Withholding Tax/Bank Charges	533-4	50	x
Compulsory Contributions(Deductions)	502	x	
Cash/Bank	100/105	x	50
Total		**50**	**50**

Prepared By   Approved By

Payment Voucher (Cash\Bank)

Date : __April 13, 2016__

Payee : _____ Voucher No: 2009

Rupees: __400/-__ Cheque No.

Particulars	A\C No.	Debit	Credit
Teachers' Salary	500		x
Other Staff Salaries	501		x
Compulsary Contributions	502		x
Overtime Payment	503		x
Water/Electricity Expenses	506-7		x
Gas/Internet and Telephone	508-9		x
Rent/Insurance/S.S. Charges	510-2		x
Capital Equipment/Vehicle	515-16		x
Repairs Building/Furniture	517-8		x
Repairs Equipment/Vehicle	519-20		x
Statioery and Printing Expenses	521		x
Postage and Revenue Expenses	522		x
Office Expenses	524		x
Transportation Expenses	525		x
Training /News paper	526-7	400	x
Expense of Lab/Sports and Functions	528-9		x
Compulsary Contributions(Deductions)	502	x	
Cash/Bank	100/105	x	400
Total		**400**	**400**

Prepared By   Approved By

Payment Voucher (Cash\Bank)

Date : __April 12, 2016__

Payee : _____ Voucher No: 2008

Rupees: __100/-__ Cheque No.

Particulars	A\C No.	Debit	Credit
Teachers' Salary	500		x
Other Staff Salaries	501		x
Compulsary Contributions	502		x
Overtime Payment	503		x
Water/Electricity Expenses	506-7		x
Gas/Internet and Telephone	508-9		x
Rent/Insurance/S.S. Charges	510-2		x
Capital Equipment/Vehicle	515-16		x
Repairs Building/Furniture	517-8		x
Repairs Equipment/Vehicle	519-20		x
Statioery and Printing Expenses	521		x
Postage and Revenue Expenses	522	100	x
Office Expenses	524		x
Transportation Expenses	525		x
Training /News paper	526-7		x
Expense of Lab/Sports and Functions	528-9		x
Compulsary Contributions(Deductions)	502	x	
Cash/Bank	100/105	x	100
Total		**100**	**100**

Prepared By   Approved By

Payment Voucher (Cash\Bank)

Date : __April 11, 2016__

Payee : _____ Voucher No: 2007

Rupees: __500/-__ Cheque No.

Particulars	A\C No.	Debit	Credit
Teachers' Salary	500		x
Other Staff Salaries	501		x
Compulsary Contributions	502		x
Overtime Payment	503		x
Water/Electricity Expenses	506-7		x
Gas/Internet and Telephone	508-9		x
Rent/Insurance/S.S. Charges	510-2		x
Capital Equipment/Vehicle	515-16		x
Repairs Building/Furniture	517-8		x
Repairs Equipment/Vehicle	519-20		x
Statioery and Printing Expenses	521		x
Postage and Revenue Expenses	522		x
Office Expenses	524		x
Transportation Expenses	525	500	x
Training /News paper	526-7		x
Expense of Lab/Sports and Functions	528-9		x
Compulsary Contributions(Deductions)	502	x	
Cash/Bank	100/105	x	500
Total		**500**	**500**

Prepared By   Approved By

Payment Voucher (Cash\Bank)

Date : _____

Payee : _____ Voucher No: 2012

Rupees: _____ Cheque No.

Particulars	A\C No.	Debit	Credit
Teachers' Salary	500		x
Other Staff Salaries	501		x
Compulsary Contributions	502		x
Overtime Payment	503		x
Water/Electricity Expenses	506-7		x
Gas/Internet and Telephone	508-9		x
Rent/Insurance/S.S. Charges	510-2		x
Capital Building/Furniture	513-4		x
Capital Equipment/Vehicle	515-16		x
Repairs Building/Furniture	517-8		x
Statioery and Printing Expenses	521		x
Postage and Revenue Expenses	522		x
Teaching Material	523		x
Office Expenses	524		x
Transportation Expenses	525		x
Training /News paper	526-7		x
Compulsary Contributions(Deductions)	502	x	
Cash/Bank	100/105	x	
Total			

Payment Voucher (Cash\Bank)

Date : __April 15, 2016__

Payee : _____ Voucher No: 2011

Rupees: __500/-__ Cheque No.

Particulars	A\C No.	Debit	Credit
Teachers' Salary	500		x
Other Staff Salaries	501		x
Compulsary Contributions	502		x
Overtime Payment	503		x
Water/Electricity Expenses	506-7		x
Gas/Internet and Telephone	508-9		x
Rent/Insurance/S.S. Charges	510-2		x
Capital Building/Furniture	513-4		x
Capital Equipment/Vehicle	515-16		x
Repairs Building/Furniture	517-8		x
Statioery and Printing Expenses	521		x
Postage and Revenue Expenses	522		x
Teaching Material	523		x
Office Expenses	524		x
Transportation Expenses	525		x
Withholding Tax/Bank Charges	533-4	500	x
Compulsary Contributions(Deductions)	502	x	
Cash/Bank	100/105	x	500
Total		**500**	**500**

Payment Voucher (Cash\Bank)

Date : __April 14, 2016__

Payee : _____ Voucher No: 2010

Rupees: __1,500/-__ Cheque No.

Particulars	A\C No.	Debit	Credit
Teachers' Salary	500		x
Other Staff Salaries	501		x
Compulsary Contributions	502		x
Overtime Payment	503		x
Water/Electricity Expenses	506-7		x
Gas/Internet and Telephone	508-9	1500	x
Rent/Insurance/S.S. Charges	510-2		x
Capital Building/Furniture	513-4		x
Capital Equipment/Vehicle	515-16		x
Repairs Building/Furniture	517-8		x
Statioery and Printing Expenses	521		x
Postage and Revenue Expenses	522		x
Teaching Material	523		x
Office Expenses	524		x
Transportation Expenses	525		x
Training /News paper	526-7		x
Compulsary Contributions(Deductions)	502	x	
Cash/Bank	100/105	x	1500
Total		**1500**	**1500**

Exercise 3

The following receipt vouchers will be prepared against each financial activity.

Receipt Voucher (Cash\Bank)

Date : April 20, 2016
Payee : _____ Voucher No 1018
Rupees: 1,500/- Cheque No.

Particulars	A\C No.	Debit	Credit
Cash	100	1500	x
Bank	105		x
To Student Registration Fee	800	x	
To Admission Fees	801	x	
To Tuition Fees	802	x	1000
To Exam Fees	803	x	
To Annual/Student Fund	804	x	400
To Misc. Charges	805	x	100
To Income from Sales	806	x	
To Interest On Saving	807	x	
To Interest on Investment	808	x	
To Grants/Donations Congre	809	x	
To Grants/Donations DBE	810	x	
To Diocese Contribution	811	x	
To Other Donations	812	x	
To Income from Org. Activites	813	x	
To Other Income	814	x	
To Others	815	x	
		x	
		x	
		x	
Total		1500	1500

Prepared By   Approved By

Receipt Voucher (Cash\Bank)

Date : April 19, 2016
Payee : _____ Voucher No 1017
Rupees: 1,500/- Cheque No.

Particulars	A\C No.	Debit	Credit
Cash	100	1500	x
Bank	105		x
To Student Registration Fee	800	x	
To Admission Fees	801	x	500
To Tuition Fees	802	x	500
To Exam Fees	803	x	
To Annual/Student Fund	804	x	400
To Misc. Charges	805	x	100
To Income from Sales	806	x	
To Interest On Saving	807	x	
To Interest on Investment	808	x	
To Grants/Donations Congre	809	x	
To Grants/Donations DBE	810	x	
To Diocese Contribution	811	x	
To Other Donations	812	x	
To Income from Org. Activites	813	x	
To Other Income	814	x	
To Others	815	x	
		x	
		x	
		x	
Total		1500	1500

Prepared By   Approved By

Receipt Voucher (Cash\Bank)

Date : April 18, 2016
Payee : _____ Voucher No 1016
Rupees: 1,300/- Cheque No.

Particulars	A\C No.	Debit	Credit
Cash	100	1300	x
Bank	105		x
To Student Registration Fee	800	x	
To Admission Fees	801	x	
To Tuition Fees	802	x	500
To Exam Fees	803	x	
To Annual/Student Fund	804	x	400
To Misc. Charges	805	x	400
To Income from Sales	806	x	
To Interest On Saving	807	x	
To Interest on Investment	808	x	
To Grants/Donations Congre	809	x	
To Grants/Donations DBE	810	x	
To Diocese Contribution	811	x	
To Other Donations	812	x	
To Income from Org. Activites	813	x	
To Other Income	814	x	
To Others	815	x	
		x	
		x	
		x	
Total		1300	1300

Prepared By   Approved By

Receipt Voucher (Cash\Bank)

Date : April 25, 2016
Payee : _____ Voucher No 1021
Rupees: 1,000/- Cheque No.

Particulars	A\C No.	Debit	Credit
Cash	100	1000	x
Bank	105		x
To Student Registration Fee	800	x	
To Admission Fees	801	x	
To Tuition Fees	802	x	500
To Exam Fees	803	x	
To Annual/Student Fund	804	x	400
To Misc. Charges	805	x	100
To Income from Sales	806	x	
To Interest On Saving	807	x	
To Interest on Investment	808	x	
To Grants/Donations Congre	809	x	
To Grants/Donations DBE	810	x	
To Diocese Contribution	811	x	
To Other Donations	812	x	
To Income from Org. Activites	813	x	
To Other Income	814	x	
To Others	815	x	
		x	
		x	
Total		1000	1000

Prepared By   Approved By

Receipt Voucher (Cash\Bank)

Date : April 22, 2016
Payee : _____ Voucher No 1020
Rupees: 2,000/- Cheque No.

Particulars	A\C No.	Debit	Credit
Cash	100	2000	x
Bank	105		x
To Student Registration Fee	800	x	
To Admission Fees	801	x	
To Tuition Fees	802	x	1000
To Exam Fees	803	x	
To Annual/Student Fund	804	x	800
To Misc. Charges	805	x	200
To Income from Sales	806	x	
To Interest On Saving	807	x	
To Interest on Investment	808	x	
To Grants/Donations Congre	809	x	
To Grants/Donations DBE	810	x	
To Diocese Contribution	811	x	
To Other Donations	812	x	
To Income from Org. Activites	813	x	
To Other Income	814	x	
To Others	815	x	
		x	
		x	
		x	
Total		2000	2000

Prepared By   Approved By

Receipt Voucher (Cash\Bank)

Date : April 21, 2016
Payee : _____ Voucher No 1019
Rupees: 3,000/- Cheque No.

Particulars	A\C No.	Debit	Credit
Cash	100	3000	x
Bank	105		x
To Student Registration Fee	800	x	
To Admission Fees	801	x	
To Tuition Fees	802	x	1500
To Exam Fees	803	x	
To Annual/Student Fund	804	x	400
To Misc. Charges	805	x	100
To Income from Sales	806	x	1000
To Interest On Saving	807	x	
To Interest on Investment	808	x	
To Grants/Donations Congre	809	x	
To Grants/Donations DBE	810	x	
To Diocese Contribution	811	x	
To Other Donations	812	x	
To Income from Org. Activites	813	x	
To Other Income	814	x	
To Others	815	x	
		x	
		x	
		x	
Total		3000	3000

Prepared By   Approved By

Receipt Voucher (Cash\Bank)

Date: April 28, 2016 — Voucher No 1024 — Cheque No. — Rupees: 1,000/-

Particulars	A\C No.	Debit	Credit
Cash	100	1000	x
Bank	105		x
To Student Registration Fee	800	x	
To Admission Fees	801	x	
To Tuition Fees	802	x	500
To Exam Fees	803	x	
To Annual/Student Fund	804	x	400
To Misc. Charges	805	x	100
To Income from Sales	806	x	
To Interest On Saving	807	x	
To Interest on Investment	808	x	
To Grants/Donations Congre	809	x	
To Grants/Donations DBE	810	x	
To Diocese Contribution	811	x	
To Other Donations	812	x	
To Income from Org. Activities	813	x	
To Other Income	814	x	
To Others	815	x	
		x	
		x	
		x	
Total		1000	1000

Prepared By — Approved By

Receipt Voucher (Cash\Bank)

Date: April 27, 2016 — Voucher No 1023 — Cheque No. — Rupees: 20,000/-

Particulars	A\C No.	Debit	Credit
Cash	100		x
Bank	105	20000	x
To Student Registration Fee	800	x	
To Admission Fees	801	x	
To Tuition Fees	802	x	
To Exam Fees	803	x	
To Annual/Student Fund	804	x	
To Misc. Charges	805	x	
To Income from Sales	806	x	
To Interest On Saving	807	x	
To Interest on Investment	808	x	
To Grants/Donations Congre	809	x	
To Grants/Donations DBE	810	x	
To Diocese Contribution	811	x	
To Other Donations	812	x	20000
To Income from Org. Activities	813	x	
To Other Income	814	x	
To Others	815	x	
		x	
		x	
		x	
Total		20000	20000

Prepared By — Approved By

Receipt Voucher (Cash\Bank)

Date: April 26, 2016 — Voucher No 1022 — Cheque No. — Rupees: 1,000/-

Particulars	A\C No.	Debit	Credit
Cash	100	1000	x
Bank	105		x
To Student Registration Fee	800	x	
To Admission Fees	801	x	
To Tuition Fees	802	x	500
To Exam Fees	803	x	
To Annual/Student Fund	804	x	400
To Misc. Charges	805	x	100
To Income from Sales	806	x	
To Interest On Saving	807	x	
To Interest on Investment	808	x	
To Grants/Donations Congre	809	x	
To Grants/Donations DBE	810	x	
To Diocese Contribution	811	x	
To Other Donations	812	x	
To Income from Org. Activities	813	x	
To Other Income	814	x	
To Others	815	x	
		x	
		x	
		x	
Total		1000	1000

Prepared By — Approved By

Receipt Voucher (Cash\Bank)

Date: April 30, 2016 — Voucher No 1027 — Cheque No. — Rupees: 600/-

Particulars	A\C No.	Debit	Credit
Cash	100		x
Bank	105	600	x
To Student Registration Fee	800	x	
To Admission Fees	801	x	
To Tuition Fees	802	x	
To Exam Fees	803	x	
To Annual/Student Fund	804	x	
To Misc. Charges	805	x	
To Income from Sales	806	x	
To Interest On Saving	807	x	600
To Interest on Investment	808	x	
To Grants/Donations Congre	809	x	
To Grants/Donations DBE	810	x	
To Diocese Contribution	811	x	
To Other Donations	812	x	
To Income from Org. Activities	813	x	
To Other Income	814	x	
To Others	815	x	
		x	
		x	
		x	
Total		600	600

Prepared By — Approved By

Receipt Voucher (Cash\Bank)

Date: April 29, 2016 — Voucher No 1026 — Cheque No. — Rupees: 50,000/-

Particulars	A\C No.	Debit	Credit
Cash	100	50000	x
Bank	105		x
To Student Registration Fee	800	x	
To Admission Fees	801	x	
To Tuition Fees	802	x	
To Exam Fees	803	x	
To Annual/Student Fund	804	x	
To Misc. Charges	805	x	
To Income from Sales	806	x	
To Interest On Saving	807	x	
To Interest on Investment	808	x	
To Grants/Donations Congre	809	x	
To Grants/Donations DBE	810	x	
To Diocese Contribution	811	x	
To Other Donations	812	x	
To Income from Org. Activities	813	x	
To Other Income	814	x	
To Others	815	x	
		x	
To Bank		x	50000
Total		50000	50000

Prepared By — Approved By

Receipt Voucher (Cash\Bank)

Date: April 29, 2016 — Voucher No 1025 — Cheque No. — Rupees: 4,000/-

Particulars	A\C No.	Debit	Credit
Cash	100	4000	x
Bank	105		x
To Student Registration Fee	800	x	
To Admission Fees	801	x	1000
To Tuition Fees	802	x	1500
To Exam Fees	803	x	
To Annual/Student Fund	804	x	1200
To Misc. Charges	805	x	300
To Income from Sales	806	x	
To Interest On Saving	807	x	
To Interest on Investment	808	x	
To Grants/Donations Congre	809	x	
To Grants/Donations DBE	810	x	
To Diocese Contribution	811	x	
To Other Donations	812	x	
To Income from Org. Activities	813	x	
To Other Income	814	x	
To Others	815	x	
		x	
		x	
		x	
Total		4000	4000

Prepared By — Approved By

Exercise 4

The following payment vouchers will be prepared against each financial activity.

Payment Voucher (Cash\Bank)			
Date : April 19, 2016			
Payee : _____		Voucher No	2013
Rupees: 3,000/-		Cheque No.	
Particulars	**A\C No.**	**Debit**	**Credit**
Teachers' Salary	500		x
Other Staff Salaries	501		x
Compulsary Contributions	502		x
Overtime Payment	503		x
Water/Electricity Expenses	506-7		x
Gas/Internet and Telephone	508-9		x
Rent/Insurance/S.S. Charges	510-2		x
Capital Building/Furniture	513-4		x
Capital Equipment/Vehicle	515-16		x
Repairs Building/Furniture	517-8		x
Repairs Equipment/Vehicle	519-20		x
Statioery and Printing Expenses	521		x
Postage and Revenue Expenses	522		x
Teaching Material	523		x
Office Expenses	524	3000	x
Transportation Expenses	525		x
Training /News paper	526-7		x
Expense of Lab/Sports and Functions	528-9		x
Withholding Tax/Bank Charges	533-4		x
Others			x
Compulsary Contributions(Deductions)	502	x	
Cash/Bank	100/105	x	3000
Total		**3000**	**3000**

Prepared By   Approved By

Payment Voucher (Cash\Bank)			
Date : April 18, 2016			
Payee : _____		Voucher No	2012
Rupees: 1,000/-		Cheque No.	
Particulars	**A\C No.**	**Debit**	**Credit**
Teachers' Salary	500		x
Other Staff Salaries	501		x
Compulsary Contributions	502		x
Overtime Payment	503		x
Water/Electricity Expenses	506-7		x
Gas/Internet and Telephone	508-9		x
Rent/Insurance/S.S. Charges	510-2		x
Capital Building/Furniture	513-4		x
Capital Equipment/Vehicle	515-16		x
Repairs Building/Furniture	517-8		x
Repairs Equipment/Vehicle	519-20		x
Statioery and Printing Expenses	521	1000	x
Postage and Revenue Expenses	522		x
Teaching Material	523		x
Office Expenses	524		x
Transportation Expenses	525		x
Training /News paper	526-7		x
Expense of Lab/Sports and Functions	528-9		x
Withholding Tax/Bank Charges	533-4		x
Others			x
Compulsary Contributions(Deductions)	502	x	
Cash/Bank	100/105	x	1000
Total		**1000**	**1000**

Prepared By   Approved By

Payment Voucher (Cash\Bank)			
Date : April 21, 2016			
Payee : _____		Voucher No	2015
Rupees: 10,000/-		Cheque No.	
Particulars	**A\C No.**	**Debit**	**Credit**
Teachers' Salary	500		x
Other Staff Salaries	501		x
Compulsary Contributions	502		x
Overtime Payment	503		x
Water/Electricity Expenses	506-7		x
Gas/Internet and Telephone	508-9		x
Rent/Insurance/S.S. Charges	510-2		x
Capital Building/Furniture	513-4	10000	x
Capital Equipment/Vehicle	515-16		x
Repairs Building/Furniture	517-8		x
Repairs Equipment/Vehicle	519-20		x
Statioery and Printing Expenses	521		x
Postage and Revenue Expenses	522		x
Teaching Material	523		x
Office Expenses	524		x
Transportation Expenses	525		x
Training /News paper	526-7		x
Expense of Lab/Sports and Functions	528-9		x
Withholding Tax/Bank Charges	533-4		x
Others			x
Compulsary Contributions(Deductions)	502	x	
Cash/Bank	100/105	x	10000
Total		**10000**	**10000**

Prepared By   Approved By

Payment Voucher (Cash\Bank)			
Date : April 20, 2016			
Payee : _____		Voucher No	2014
Rupees: 1,000/-		Cheque No.	
Particulars	**A\C No.**	**Debit**	**Credit**
Teachers' Salary	500		x
Other Staff Salaries	501		x
Compulsary Contributions	502		x
Overtime Payment	503		x
Water/Electricity Expenses	506-7		x
Gas/Internet and Telephone	508-9	1000	x
Rent/Insurance/S.S. Charges	510-2		x
Capital Building/Furniture	513-4		x
Capital Equipment/Vehicle	515-16		x
Repairs Building/Furniture	517-8		x
Repairs Equipment/Vehicle	519-20		x
Statioery and Printing Expenses	521		x
Postage and Revenue Expenses	522		x
Teaching Material	523		x
Office Expenses	524		x
Transportation Expenses	525		x
Training /News paper	526-7		x
Expense of Lab/Sports and Functions	528-9		x
Withholding Tax/Bank Charges	533-4		x
Others			x
Compulsary Contributions(Deductions)	502	x	
Cash/Bank	100/105	x	1000
Total		**1000**	**1000**

Prepared By   Approved By

Payment Voucher (Cash\Bank)			
Date : April 25, 2016			
Payee : _____		Voucher No	2017
Rupees: 10,000/-		Cheque No.	
Particulars	**A\C No.**	**Debit**	**Credit**
Teachers' Salary	500		x
Other Staff Salaries	501		x
Compulsary Contributions	502		x
Overtime Payment	503		x
Water/Electricity Expenses	506-7		x
Gas/Internet and Telephone	508-9		x
Rent/Insurance/S.S. Charges	510-2		x
Capital Building/Furniture	513-4		x
Capital Equipment/Vehicle	515-16	10000	x
Repairs Building/Furniture	517-8		x
Repairs Equipment/Vehicle	519-20		x
Statioery and Printing Expenses	521		x
Postage and Revenue Expenses	522		x
Teaching Material	523		x
Office Expenses	524		x
Transportation Expenses	525		x
Training /News paper	526-7		x
Expense of Lab/Sports and Functions	528-9		x
Withholding Tax/Bank Charges	533-4		x
Others			x
Compulsary Contributions(Deductions)	502	x	
Cash/Bank	100/105	x	10000
Total		**10000**	**10000**

Prepared By   Approved By

Payment Voucher (Cash\Bank)			
Date : April 22, 2016			
Payee : _____		Voucher No	2016
Rupees: 2,000/-		Cheque No.	
Particulars	**A\C No.**	**Debit**	**Credit**
Teachers' Salary	500		x
Other Staff Salaries	501		x
Compulsary Contributions	502		x
Overtime Payment	503		x
Water/Electricity Expenses	506-7		x
Gas/Internet and Telephone	508-9		x
Rent/Insurance/S.S. Charges	510-2		x
Capital Building/Furniture	513-4		x
Capital Equipment/Vehicle	515-16		x
Repairs Building/Furniture	517-8	2000	x
Repairs Equipment/Vehicle	519-20		x
Statioery and Printing Expenses	521		x
Postage and Revenue Expenses	522		x
Teaching Material	523		x
Office Expenses	524		x
Transportation Expenses	525		x
Training /News paper	526-7		x
Expense of Lab/Sports and Functions	528-9		x
Withholding Tax/Bank Charges	533-4		x
Others			x
Compulsary Contributions(Deductions)	502	x	
Cash/Bank	100/105	x	2000
Total		**2000**	**2000**

Prepared By   Approved By

<table>
<tr><td colspan="4">

Payment Voucher (Cash\Bank)

Date : __April 27, 2016__

Payee : _____ Voucher No   2019

Rupees: 1,500/- Cheque No.

</td></tr>
</table>

Particulars	A\C No.	Debit	Credit
Teachers' Salary	500		x
Other Staff Salaries	501		x
Compulsary Contributions	502		x
Overtime Payment	503		x
Water/Electricity Expenses	506-7		x
Gas/Internet and Telephone	508-9		x
Rent/Insurance/S.S. Charges	510-2		x
Capital Building/Furniture	513-4	1500	x
Capital Equipment/Vehicle	515-16		x
Repairs Building/Furniture	517-8		x
Repairs Equipment/Vehicle	519-20		x
Statioery and Printing Expenses	521		x
Postage and Revenue Expenses	522		x
Teaching Material	523		x
Office Expenses	524		x
Transportation Expenses	525		x
Training /News paper	526-7		x
Expense of Lab/Sports and Functions	528-9		x
Withholding Tax/Bank Charges	533-4		x
Others			x
Compulsary Contributions(Deductions)	502	x	
Cash/Bank	100/105	x	1500
Total		**1500**	**1500**

Prepared By   Approved By

<table>
<tr><td colspan="4">

Payment Voucher (Cash\Bank)

Date : __April 26, 2016__

Payee : _____ Voucher No   2018

Rupees: 1,000/- Cheque No.

</td></tr>
</table>

Particulars	A\C No.	Debit	Credit
Teachers' Salary	500		x
Other Staff Salaries	501		x
Compulsary Contributions	502		x
Overtime Payment	503		x
Water/Electricity Expenses	506-7		x
Gas/Internet and Telephone	508-9		x
Rent/Insurance/S.S. Charges	510-2		x
Capital Building/Furniture	513-4		x
Capital Equipment/Vehicle	515-16		x
Repairs Building/Furniture	517-8		x
Repairs Equipment/Vehicle	519-20		x
Statioery and Printing Expenses	521		x
Postage and Revenue Expenses	522		x
Teaching Material	523		x
Office Expenses	524		x
Transportation Expenses	525	1000	x
Training /News paper	526-7		x
Expense of Lab/Sports and Functions	528-9		x
Withholding Tax/Bank Charges	533-4		x
Others			x
Compulsary Contributions(Deductions)	502	x	
Cash/Bank	100/105	x	1000
Total		**1000**	**1000**

Prepared By   Approved By

Payment Voucher (Cash\Bank)			
Date : April 30, 2016			
Payee : _____		Voucher No 2022	
Rupees: 60/-		Cheque No.	

Particulars	A\C No.	Debit	Credit
Teachers' Salary	500		x
Other Staff Salaries	501		x
Compulsory Contributions	502		x
Overtime Payment	503		x
Water/Electricity Expenses	506-7		x
Gas/Internet and Telephone	508-9		x
Rent/Insurance/S.S. Charges	510-2		x
Capital Building/Furniture	513-4		x
Capital Equipment/Vehicle	515-16		x
Repairs Building/Furniture	517-8		x
Repairs Equipment/Vehicle	519-20		x
Stationery and Printing Expenses	521		x
Postage and Revenue Expenses	522		x
Teaching Material	523		x
Office Expenses	524		x
Transportation Expenses	525		x
Training /News paper	526-7		x
Expense of Lab/Sports and Functions	528-9		x
Withholding Tax/Bank Charges	533-4	60	x
Others			x
Compulsory Contributions(Deductions)	502	x	
Cash/Bank	100/105	x	60
Total		**60**	**60**

Prepared By   Approved By

Payment Voucher (Cash\Bank)			
Date : April 29, 2016			
Payee : _____		Voucher No 2021	
Rupees: 4,500/-		Cheque No.	

Particulars	A\C No.	Debit	Credit
Teachers' Salary	500		x
Other Staff Salaries	501		x
Compulsory Contributions	502	4500	x
Overtime Payment	503		x
Water/Electricity Expenses	506-7		x
Gas/Internet and Telephone	508-9		x
Rent/Insurance/S.S. Charges	510-2		x
Capital Building/Furniture	513-4		x
Capital Equipment/Vehicle	515-16		x
Repairs Building/Furniture	517-8		x
Repairs Equipment/Vehicle	519-20		x
Statioery and Printing Expenses	521		x
Postage and Revenue Expenses	522		x
Teaching Material	523		x
Office Expenses	524		x
Transportation Expenses	525		x
Training /News paper	526-7		x
Expense of Lab/Sports and Functions	528-9		x
Withholding Tax/Bank Charges	533-4		x
Others			x
Compulsory Contributions(Deductions)	502	x	
Cash/Bank	100/105	x	4500
Total		**4500**	**4500**

Prepared By   Approved By

Payment Voucher (Cash\Bank)			
Date : April 28, 2016			
Payee : _____		Voucher No 2020	
Rupees: 58,880/-		Cheque No.	

Particulars	A\C No.	Debit	Credit
Teachers' Salary	500	49200	x
Other Staff Salaries	501	9600	x
Compulsory Contributions	502		x
Overtime Payment	503		x
Water/Electricity Expenses	506-7		x
Gas/Internet and Telephone	508-9		x
Rent/Insurance/S.S. Charges	510-2		x
Capital Building/Furniture	513-4		x
Capital Equipment/Vehicle	515-16		x
Repairs Building/Furniture	517-8		x
Repairs Equipment/Vehicle	519-20		x
Stationery and Printing Expenses	521		x
Postage and Revenue Expenses	522		x
Teaching Material	523		x
Office Expenses	524		x
Transportation Expenses	525		x
Training /News paper	526-7		x
Expense of Lab/Sports and Functions	528-9		x
Withholding Tax/Bank Charges	533-4		x
Others			x
Compulsory Contributions(Deductions)	502	x	2770
Cash/Bank	100/105	x	56030
Total		**58800**	**58800**

Prepared By   Approved By

Chapter Five – Step 3 Classifying or Posting the Financial Activity

In the previous chapter, with the help of the source document we have been able to record the financial activities, now we are in stage which is far more easy then the previous one because in this step we just post the entries in the respective ledger accounts and that's it. How we are going to do this is indicated below:

Exercise 1 - 4

We have transferred the balances of the entries from all four exercises (April 01 – 30, 2016) in the respective ledgers which is shown below:

800 Registration Fee

Date	Particulars	Vr. #	Debit	Credit	Dr. or Cr.	Balance
1-Apr	Cash	1001		500	Cr.	500
	Monthly Total		0	500		

801 Admission Fee

Date	Particulars	Vr. #	Debit	Credit	Dr. or Cr.	Balance
1-Apr	Cash	1001		500	Cr.	500
12-Apr	Cash	1009		500	Cr.	1000
15-Apr	Cash	1013		500	Cr.	1500
19-Apr	Cash	1017		500	Cr.	2000
29-Apr	Cash	1025		1000	Cr.	3000
	Monthly Total		0	3000		

802 Tuition Fee

Date	Particulars	Vr. #	Debit	Credit	Dr. or Cr.	Balance
1-Apr	Cash	1001		1000	Cr.	1000
4-Apr	Cash	1002		2500	Cr.	3500
6-Apr	Cash	1004		500	Cr.	4000
7-Apr	Cash	1005		500	Cr.	4500
8-Apr	Cash	1006		1000	Cr.	5500
11-Apr	Cash	1008		500	Cr.	6000
12-Apr	Cash	1009		500	Cr.	6500
14-Apr	Cash	1011		500	Cr.	7000
15-Apr	Cash	1013		500	Cr.	7500
18-Apr	Cash	1016		500	Cr.	8000
19-Apr	Cash	1017		500	Cr.	8500

804 Annual Fund

Date	Particulars	Vr. #	Debit	Credit	Dr. or Cr.	Balance
1-Apr	Cash	1001		800	Cr.	800
4-Apr	Cash	1002		800	Cr.	1600
6-Apr	Cash	1004		400	Cr.	2000
7-Apr	Cash	1005		400	Cr.	2400
8-Apr	Cash	1006		800	Cr.	3200
11-Apr	Cash	1008		400	Cr.	3600
12-Apr	Cash	1009		400	Cr.	4000
14-Apr	Cash	1011		400	Cr.	4400
15-Apr	Cash	1013		400	Cr.	4800
18-Apr	Cash	1016		400	Cr.	5200
19-Apr	Cash	1017		400	Cr.	5600

Date	Particulars	Vr. #	Debit	Credit	Dr. or Cr.	Balance		Date	Particulars	Vr. #	Debit	Credit	Dr. or Cr.	Balance
20-Apr	Cash	1018		1000	Cr.	9500		20-Apr	Cash	1018		400	Cr.	6000
21-Apr	Cash	1019		1500	Cr.	11000		21-Apr	Cash	1019		400	Cr.	6400
22-Apr	Cash	1020		1000	Cr.	12000		22-Apr	Cash	1020		800	Cr.	7200
25-Apr	Cash	1021		500	Cr.	12500		25-Apr	Cash	1021		400	Cr.	7600
26-Apr	Cash	1022		500	Cr.	13000		26-Apr	Cash	1022		400	Cr.	8000
28-Apr	Cash	1024		500	Cr.	13500		28-Apr	Cash	1024		400	Cr.	8400
29-Apr	Cash	1025		1500	Cr.	15000		29-Apr	Cash	1025		1200	Cr.	9600
	Monthly Total		0	15000					Monthly Total		0	9600		

805 Misc. Charges

Date	Particulars	Vr. #	Debit	Credit	Dr. or Cr.	Balance
1-Apr	Cash	1001		700	Cr.	700
4-Apr	Cash	1002		200	Cr.	900
6-Apr	Cash	1004		100	Cr.	1000
7-Apr	Cash	1005		100	Cr.	1100
8-Apr	Cash	1006		200	Cr.	1300
11-Apr	Cash	1008		100	Cr.	1400
12-Apr	Cash	1009		100	Cr.	1500
14-Apr	Cash	1011		100	Cr.	1600
15-Apr	Cash	1013		100	Cr.	1700
18-Apr	Cash	1016		400	Cr.	2100
19-Apr	Cash	1017		100	Cr.	2200
20-Apr	Cash	1018		100	Cr.	2300
21-Apr	Cash	1019		100	Cr.	2400
22-Apr	Cash	1020		200	Cr.	2600
25-Apr	Cash	1021		100	Cr.	2700
26-Apr	Cash	1022		100	Cr.	2800
28-Apr	Cash	1024		100	Cr.	2900
29-Apr	Cash	1025		300	Cr.	3200
	Monthly Total		0	8500		

806 Income from Sales and Provident Services

Date	Particulars	Vr. #	Debit	Credit	Dr. or Cr.	Balance
5-Apr	Cash(Canteen Rent)	1003		2000	Cr.	2000
13-Apr	Bank(Generator Sold)	1010		1000	Cr.	3000
21-Apr	Cash(Diaries)	1019		1000	Cr.	4000
	Monthly Total		0	4000		

807 Interest on Bank Saving Account

Date	Particulars	Vr. #	Debit	Credit	Dr. or Cr.	Balance
30-Apr	Bank	1027		600	Cr.	600
	Monthly Total		0	600		

808 Interest on Investment

Date	Particulars	Vr. #	Debit	Credit	Dr. or Cr.	Balance
15-Apr	Bank	1014		5000	Cr.	5000
	Monthly Total		0	5000		

810 DBE Contribution

Date	Particulars	Vr. #	Debit	Credit	Dr. or Cr.	Balance
11-Apr	Bank	1007		10000	Cr.	10000
	Monthly Total		0	10000		

812 Other Donations

Date	Particulars	Vr. #	Debit	Credit	Dr. or Cr.	Balance
27-Apr	Bank	1023		20000	Cr.	20000
	Monthly Total		0	20000		

500 Teachers' Salaries

Date	Particulars	Vr. #	Debit	Credit	Dr. or Cr.	Balance
28-Apr	Salaries for April 2016	2020	49200		Dr.	49200
	Monthly Total		49200	0		

501 Non - Teachers' Salaries

Date	Particulars	Vr. #	Debit	Credit	Dr. or Cr.	Balance
28-Apr	Salaries for April 2016	2020	9600		Dr.	9600
	Monthly Total		9600	0		

502 Contributions towards EOBI, F.P etc.

Date	Particulars	Vr. #	Debit	Credit	Dr. or Cr.	Balance
5-Apr	Cash	2003	2600		Dr.	2600

503 Overtime Payment

Date	Particulars	Vr. #	Debit	Credit	Dr. or Cr.	Balance
1-Apr	Cash	2001	1500		Dr.	1500

Date	Particulars	Vr. #	Debit	Credit	Dr. or Cr.	Balance
28-Apr	Salaries for April 2016	2020		520	Dr.	2080
28-Apr	Salaries for April 2016	2020		2250	Cr.	-170
29-Apr	Bank	2021	4500		Dr.	4330
	Monthly Total		7100	2770		

Date	Particulars	Vr. #	Debit	Credit	Dr. or Cr.	Balance
	Monthly Total		1500	0		

506 Electricity Bill

Date	Particulars	Vr. #	Debit	Credit	Dr. or Cr.	Balance
8-Apr	Cash	2006	3000		Dr.	3000
	Monthly Total		3000	0		

508 Gas Bill

Date	Particulars	Vr. #	Debit	Credit	Dr. or Cr.	Balance
20-Apr	Cash	2014	1000		Dr.	1000
	Monthly Total		1000	0		

509 Telephone / Internet

Date	Particulars	Vr. #	Debit	Credit	Dr. or Cr.	Balance
14-Apr	Cash	2010	1500		Dr.	1500
	Monthly Total		1500	0		

511 Furniture and Fittings

Date	Particulars	Vr. #	Debit	Credit	Dr. or Cr.	Balance
21-Apr	Cash	2015	10000		Dr.	10000
	Monthly Total		10000	0		

515 Equipment and Teaching Aid

Date	Particulars	Vr. #	Debit	Credit	Dr. or Cr.	Balance
25-Apr	Cash	2017	10000		Dr.	10000
	Monthly Total		10000	0		

517 Building Repairs

Date	Particulars	Vr. #	Debit	Credit	Dr. or Cr.	Balance
22-Apr	Cash	2016	2000		Dr.	2000
	Monthly Total		2000	0		

518 Furniture and Fittings Repairs

Date	Particulars	Vr. #	Debit	Credit	Dr. or Cr.	Balance
7-Apr	Cash	2005	2000		Dr.	2000
27-Apr	Cash	2019	1500		Dr.	3500
	Monthly Total		3500	0		

521 Stationery and Printing

Date	Particulars	Vr. #	Debit	Credit	Dr. or Cr.	Balance
1-Apr	Cash	2001	2000		Dr.	2000
18-Apr	Cash	2012	1000		Dr.	3000
	Monthly Total		3000	0		

522 Postage and Revenue Expenses

Date	Particulars	Vr. #	Debit	Credit	Dr. or Cr.	Balance
12-Apr	Cash	2008	100		Dr.	100
	Monthly Total		100	0		

523 Teaching Aids

Date	Particulars	Vr. #	Debit	Credit	Dr. or Cr.	Balance
1-Apr	Cash	2002	1000		Dr.	1000
	Monthly Total		1000	0		

524 Office Expenses

Date	Particulars	Vr. #	Debit	Credit	Dr. or Cr.	Balance
1-Apr	Cash	2001	3000		Dr.	3000
19-Apr	Cash	2013	3000		Dr.	6000
	Monthly Total		6000	0		

525 Transportation Expenses

Date	Particulars	Vr. #	Debit	Credit	Dr. or Cr.	Balance
1-Apr	Cash	2007	500		Dr.	500
26-Apr	Cash	2018	1000		Dr.	1500
	Monthly Total		1500	0		

527 News Papers

Date	Particulars	Vr. #	Debit	Credit	Dr. or Cr.	Balance
13-Apr	Cash	2009	400		Dr.	400
	Monthly Total		400	0		

530 Misc. Expenses

Date	Particulars	Vr. #	Debit	Credit	Dr. or Cr.	Balance

533 Withholding Tax on Interest

Date	Particulars	Vr. #	Debit	Credit	Dr. or Cr.	Balance
15-Apr	Bank	2011	500		Dr.	500
30-Apr	Bank	2022	60		Dr.	560
	Monthly Total		560	0		

534 Bank Charges

Date	Particulars	Vr. #	Debit	Credit	Dr. or Cr.	Balance
6-Apr	Bank	2004	50		Dr.	50
	Monthly Total		50	0		

Note: Two Ledgers Cash Ledger/Book and Bank Ledger/Book are maintained separately due to the volume and importance of them in the whole accounting/book keeping process. We have therefore used these as follows:

Bank Book											
Receipts						**Payments**					
Date	Particulars	V.No.	A\C No.	Amount	Acc. Balance	Date	Particulars	V.No.	A\C No.	Amount	Acc. Balance
1-Apr	Opening Balance		105	100,000	100,000	5-Apr	Bank Charges	2004	534	50	50
11-Apr	Grant from DBE(Cheque)	1007	810	10,000	110,000	15-Apr	Withholding Tax	2011	533	500	550
13-Apr	Sale of Generator(Cheque)	1010	806	1,000	111,000	15-Apr	Cash withdrawn from Bank	1015	100	20,000	20,550
15-Apr	Interest on Investment	1014	808	5,000	116,000	29-Apr	Cash withdrawn from Bank	1026	100	50,000	70,550
27-Apr	Grant from Govt.	1023	812	20,000	136,000	29-Apr	Provident Fund Payment to CPF	2021	502	4,500	75,050
30-Apr	interest on Saving Account	1027	807	600	136,600	30-Apr	Withholding Tax	2022	533	60	75,110
					136,600						75,110

					136,600

					75,110

	Opening Balance	**100,000**
Add	Current Receipts	36,600
Subtract	Current Payments	(75,110)
	Cash Closing Balance	**61,490**

Cash Book											
Receipts						**Payments**					
Date	Particulars	V. No.	A\C No.	Amount	Acc. Balance	Date	Particulars	V. No.	A\C No.	Amount	Acc. Balance
1-Apr	Opening Balance			10,000	10,000	1-Apr	Stationery Purchased	2001	521	2,000	2,000
1-Apr	Student Registration Fees	1001	800	500	10,500	1-Apr	Refreshment (Tea, Milk etc.)	2001	524	3,000	5,000
	Admission Fee	1001	801	500	11,000	1-Apr	Overtime Payment for March 2016	2001	504	1,500	6,500
	Tuition Fee	1001	802	1,000	12,000	4-Apr	Books for School Teachers	2002	523	1,000	7,500
	Annual Fund	1001	804	800	12,800	5-Apr	EOBI Payment for March 2016	2003	502	2,600	10,100
	Misc. Charges	1001	805	700	13,500	7-Apr	Water Pump Repairing Charges	2005	518	2,000	12,100
4-Apr	Tuition Fee	1002	802	2,500	16,000	8-Apr	Electricity Bill Payment	2006	506	3,000	15,100
	Annual Fund	1002	804	800	16,800	11-Apr	Transportation Charges	2007	525	500	15,600
	Misc. Charges	1002	805	200	17,000	12-Apr	Postage Expenses	2008	522	100	15,700
5-Apr	Canteen Income	1003	806	2,000	19,000	13-Apr	News Paper	2009	527	400	16,100
6-Apr	Tuition Fee	1004	802	500	19,500	14-Apr	Telephone and Internet Expenses	2010	509	1,500	17,600
	Annual Fund	1004	804	400	19,900	18-Apr	Stationery for Teachers and Office	2012	521	1,000	18,600
	Misc. Charges	1004	805	100	20,000	19-Apr	Refreshment Expenses	2013	524	3,000	21,600
7-Apr	Tuition Fee	1005	802	500	20,500	20-Apr	Gas Bill	2014	508	1,000	22,600
	Annual Fund	1005	804	400	20,900	21-Apr	New Water Pump purchased	2015	514	10,000	32,600
	Misc. Charges	1005	805	100	21,000	22-Apr	Class Room Repairing work	2016	517	2,000	34,600
8-Apr	Tuition Fee	1006	802	1,000	22,000	25-Apr	New Computer System for Office	2017	515	10,000	44,600
	Annual Fund	1006	804	800	22,800	26-Apr	Transportation	2018	525	1,000	45,600
	Misc. Charges	1006	805	200	23,000	27-Apr	Furniture Repairing Charges	2019	518	1,500	47,100
11-Apr	Tuition Fee	1008	802	500	23,500	29-Apr	Salaries Paid to Teaching Staff	2020	500	46,935	94,035
	Annual Fund	1008	804	400	23,900	29-Apr	Salaries Paid to Non Teaching Staff	2020	501	9,095	103,130
	Misc. Charges	1008	805	100	24,000						103,130
12-Apr	Admission Fee	1009	801	500	24,500						103,130

Date	Particulars											
	Tuition Fee	1009	802	500	25,000							103,130
	Annual Fund	1009	804	400	25,400							103,130
	Misc. Charges	1009	805	100	25,500							103,130
14-Apr	Tuition Fee	1011	802	500	26,000							103,130
	Annual Fund	1011	804	400	26,400							103,130
	Misc. Charges	1011	805	100	26,500							103,130
15-Apr	Admission Fee	1013	801	500	27,000							103,130
	Tuition Fee	1013	802	500	27,500							103,130
	Annual Fund	1013	804	400	27,900							103,130
	Misc. Charges	1013	805	100	28,000							103,130
15-Apr	Cash withdrawn from Bank	1015	105	20,000	48,000							103,130
18-Apr	Tuition Fee	1016	802	500	48,500							103,130
	Annual Fund	1016	804	400	48,900							103,130
	Misc. Charges	1016	805	400	49,300							103,130
19-Apr	Admission Fee	1017	801	500	49,800							103,130
	Tuition Fee	1017	802	500	50,300							103,130
	Annual Fund	1017	807	400	50,700							103,130
	Misc. Charges	1017	805	100	50,800							103,130
20-Apr	Tuition Fee	1018	802	1,000	51,800							103,130
	Annual Fund	1018	804	400	52,200							103,130
	Misc. Charges	1018	805	100	52,300							103,130
21-Apr	Tuition Fee	1019	802	1,500	53,800							103,130
	Annual Fund	1019	804	400	54,200							103,130
	Misc. Charges	1019	805	100	54,300							103,130
	Income from Sale	1019	806	1,000	55,300							103,130
22-Apr	Tuition Fee	1020	802	1,000	56,300							103,130
	Annual Fund	1020	804	800	57,100							103,130
	Misc. Charges	1020	805	200	57,300							103,130
25-Apr	Tuition Fee	1021	802	500	57,800							103,130
	Annual Fund	1021	804	400	58,200							103,130
	Misc. Charges	1021	805	100	58,300							103,130
26-Apr	Tuition Fee	1022	802	500	58,800							103,130
	Annual Fund	1022	804	400	59,200							103,130
	Misc. Charges	1022	805	100	59,300							103,130
28-Apr	Tuition Fee	1024	802	500	59,800							103,130
	Annual Fund	1024	804	400	60,200							103,130

Date	Description											
	Misc. Charges	1024	805	100	60,300							103,130
29-Apr	Admission Fee	1025	801	1,000	61,300							103,130
	Tuition Fee	1025	802	1,500	62,800							103,130
	Annual Fund	1025	804	1,200	64,000							103,130
	Misc. Charges	1025	805	300	64,300							103,130
29-Apr	Cash Withdrawn from Bank for Salaries	1026	105	50,000	114,300							103,130
					114,300							
					114,300							
					114,300							

	Opening Balance	**10,000**	
Add	Current Receipts	104,300	
Subtract	Current Payments	(103,130)	
	Cash Closing Balance	**11,170**	

Chapter Six – Step 4 Summarizing the Transactions

We are now in a last stage of our book keeping process which is considered to be the easiest of above two steps because in this step we just need to make totals of each ledger and transfer those total to the trial balance i.e., totals of debit balances and credit balances in the trial balance. Once we have transferred all the balance into the correct columns of the trial balance against respective ledger and if the totals of the debit side of the trial balance is equal to the credit side, then we have successful complete the book keeping process. For further checks, we can use some reconciliation statements to verify the accuracy of the work.

Exercise 1 - 4

In the below trial balance, we have transferred all the ledger balances and after transferring the balances, the trial will be as follows:

FINANCIAL STATEMENT D.B.E.

School Name	Enter School Name	School Number	Enter School Code	Month:	**April**

Trial Balance

		Opening balance		Current month		Closing balance	
Account No.	**Description**	*Debit*	*Credit*	*Debit*	*Credit*	*Debit*	*Credit*
Fees and Student Contributions							
800	Students Registration Fees	0	0		500	0	500
801	Admission Fees	0	0		3,000	0	3,000
802	Tuition Fees	0	0		15,000	0	15,000
803	Exam Fees	0	0			0	0
804	Annual/Students Fund	0	0		9,600	0	9,600
805	Misc Charges	0	0		3,200	0	3,200
806	Income from Sales & Provided Services	0	0		4,000	0	4,000
Financial Income							
807	Profit/Interest on Bank Accounts	0	0		600	0	600
808	Profit/Interest on Investments	0	0		5,000	0	5,000
Grants and Donations Received							
809	Institutions or Congregations	0	0			0	0
810	DBE Contributions	0	0		10,000	0	10,000
811	Diocese Contributions	0	0			0	0
812	Other Donations	0	0		20,000	0	20,000
Misc. Income							
813	Income from Organised Activities	0	0			0	0
814	Other Income	0	0			0	0
Staff Cost							
500	Teachers' Salaries (Gross Payments)	0	0	49,200		49,200	0
501	Other Staff Salaries (Gross Payments)	0	0	9,600		9,600	0
502	Compulsory Contributions	0	0	7,100	2,770	4,330	0

503	Overtime Payments	0	0	1,500		1,500	0
504	Gratuity Payments	0	0			0	0
505	Others	0	0			0	0
Utilities							
506	Electricity	0	0	3,000		3,000	0
507	Water	0	0			0	0
508	Gas	0	0	1,000		1,000	0
509	Telephone/Internet	0	0	1,500		1,500	0
Fixed Expenses							
510	Rent	0	0			0	0
511	Insurance	0	0			0	0
512	Special School Charges and Taxes	0	0			0	0
Capital Expenditure							
513	Building	0	0			0	0
514	Furniture & Fittings	0	0	10,000		10,000	0
515	Equipment & Teaching Aids	0	0	10,000		10,000	0
516	Motor Vehicles	0	0			0	0
Repairs and Maintenance							
517	Building repairs	0	0	2,000		2,000	0
518	Furniture & fittings	0	0	3,500		3,500	0
519	Equipment & teaching aids	0	0			0	0
520	Motor vehicles	0	0			0	0
Admin. & Educational Expenses							
521	Stationary & Printing	0	0	3,000		3,000	0
522	Postage & Revenue stamps	0	0	100		100	0
523	Teaching Material	0	0	1,000		1,000	0
524	Office Expenses	0	0	6,000		6,000	0
525	Transport & Travelling	0	0	1,500		1,500	0
526	Training & Courses	0	0			0	0
527	Subscriptions of Newspapers, Magazines etc.	0	0	400		400	0
528	Expenses of Lab, Library and Computer room	0	0	0		0	0
529	Sports & Functions	0	0	0		0	0
530	Legal Service Charges	0	0	0		0	0
531	Miscellaneous Expenses	0	0	0		0	0
532	Expenses of Sales and Services	0	0	0		0	0
Financial Expenses							
533	Withholding Tax on Bank Profits/Interests	0	0	560		560	0
534	Bank Charges	0	0	50		50	0
Grants and Donations Paid							
535	Institutions or Congregations	0	0			0	0

536	DBE Contributions	0	0			0	0
537	Diocese Contributions	0	0			0	0
538	Other Donations	0	0			0	0
Current Assets							
100	Cash	10,000		104,300	103,130	11,170	0
105	**Bank name here**	100,000		36,600	75,110	61,490	0
106	**Bank name here**					0	0
107	**Bank name here**					0	0
108	**Bank name here**					0	0
109	**Bank name here**					0	0
110	**Bank name here**					0	0
115	Term Deposits & Investments					0	0
120	Account Receivables					0	0
125	Stock					0	0
Current Liabilities							
130	Account Payables					0	0
135	Withholding Tax Payable					0	0
140	Student Security Fee Payable					0	0
145	Provident Fund Loan Repayments					0	0
Capital							
	Own Capital	0	110,000			0	110,000
	Total (both sides should be equal)	**110,000**	**110,000**	**251,910**	**251,910**	**180,900**	**180,900**

As we can see from the total of the debit side of the trial balance is equal to the credit side of the trial balance, so we can say that we have been able to correctly complete the bookkeeping for the month of April 2016 using exercise 1 – 4.

<u>Reconciliation Statements</u>

Reconciliation Bank / Cash

On the last day of the month:	Cash in box	Closing bal. Cash book
Bank name here	11,170	11,170

On the last day of the month:	Bal. bank statement	Outstanding cheques	Total (Bs + OC)	Closing bal. Bank book
Bank name here	65,990	(4,500)	61,490	61,490
Bank name here			0	0
Bank name here			0	0
Bank name here			0	0
Bank name here			0	0
Term Deposits & Investments			0	0
Account Receivables			0	0

Bank statements need to be attached

Outstanding cheques

Enter Bank Name and code from previous page here

Date	No.	Description	Amount
4/29/2016	CD1111112	Provident Fund	4,500
Total outstanding cheques		*(to page 4)*	**4,500**

Enter Bank Name and code from previous page here

Total outstanding cheques		*(to page 4)*	**0**

Daily Cash Balance Overview

Date	Acc. Receipts (incl. Op. Bal.	Accumulated Payments	Cash Balance	Actual Cash in Hand	Accountant	Principal
Month:	Apr-16				Signature:	
1	13500	6500	7000	7000		
2						
3	Saturday and Sunday					
4	17000	7500	9500	9500		
5	19000	10100	8900	8900		
6	20000	10100	9900	9900		
7	21000	12100	8900	8900		
8	23000	15100	7900	7900		
9						
10	Saturday and Sunday					
11	24000	15600	8400	8400		
12	25500	15700	9800	9800		
13	25500	16100	9400	9400		
14	26500	17600	8900	8900		
15	48000	17600	30400	30400		
16						
17	Saturday and Sunday					
18	49300	18600	30700	30700		
19	50800	21600	29200	29200		
20	52300	22600	29700	29700		
21	55300	32600	22700	22700		
22	57300	34600	22700	22700		
23						
24	Saturday and Sunday					
25	58300	44600	13700	13700		
26	59300	45600	13700	13700		
27	59300	47100	12200	12200		
28	60300	47100	13200	13200		
29	114300	103130	11170	11170		
30	Saturday					

50

Salaries reconciliation form

School name & No:

Place:

School Year: 2016 – 2017

Month		Salary Register	Cash/Bank book	G. Ledger	Trial balance	Difference
April	Teaching staff	49,200	46,935	49,200	49,200	2,265
	Non-tech. staff	9,600	9,095	9,600	9,600	505
May	Teaching staff					
	Non-tech. staff					
June	Teaching staff					
	Non-tech. staff					
July	Teaching staff					
	Non-tech. staff					
August	Teaching staff					
	Non-tech. staff					
September	Teaching staff					
	Non-tech. staff					
October	Teaching staff					
	Non-tech. staff					
November	Teaching staff					
	Non-tech. staff					
December	Teaching staff					
	Non-tech. staff					
January	Teaching staff					
	Non-tech. staff					
February	Teaching staff					
	Non-tech. staff					
March	Teaching staff					
	Non-tech. staff					
Yearly total		58,800	56,030	58,800	58,800	2,770

Fee Reconciliation Statement

School Name & No: _____-_____-_____   **School Year:** 2016-2017

Months:		Fee books			Accounting books			
		Receipts	Daily fee book	Fee register	Cash book	GL	Trialbalance	Difference
April	Adm. Fee	3000	3000	3000	3000	3000	3000	0
	Tuition fee	15000	15000	15000	15000	15000	15000	0
	Annual/Student	9600	9600	9600	9600	9600	9600	0
	Misc. Charges	2400	2400	2400	3200	3200	3200	800
	Sales/Services	0	0	0	4000	4000	4000	4,000
May	Adm. Fee							
	Tuition fee							
	Annual/Student							
	Misc. Charges							
	Sales/Services							
June	Adm. Fee							
	Tuition fee							
	Annual/Student							
	Misc. Charges							
	Sales/Services							
July	Adm. Fee							
	Tuition fee							
	Annual/Student							
	Misc. Charges							
	Sales/Services							
August	Adm. Fee							
	Tuition fee							
	Annual/Student							
	Misc. Charges							
	Sales/Services							
September	Adm. Fee							
	Tuition fee							
	Annual/Student							
	Misc. Charges							
	Sales/Services							
October	Adm. Fee							
	Tuition fee							
	Annual/Student							
	Misc. Charges							
	Sales/Services							

Month	Category							
November	Adm. Fee							
	Tuition fee							
	Annual/Student							
	Misc. Charges							
	Sales/Services							
December	Adm. Fee							
	Tuition fee							
	Annual/Student							
	Misc. Charges							
	Sales/Services							
January	Adm. Fee							
	Tuition fee							
	Annual/Student							
	Misc. Charges							
	Sales/Services							
February	Adm. Fee							
	Tuition fee							
	Annual/Student							
	Misc. Charges							
	Sales/Services							
March	Adm. Fee							
	Tuition fee							
	Annual/Student							
	Misc. Charges							
	Sales/Services							
Total		30000	30000	30000	34800	34800	34800	4800

Annexure

Material for Further Practice

EXPENSE FORM D.B.E.

Name:		School/unit:			Date:			
Date	Description	Stationary/Print	Office expenses	Telephone	Petrol /Transport	Other	Total	Acc. No.
Total		-	-	-	-	-	-	

Receipts have to be attached

Checked
by: Approved by: Received by:

Expense form A

Date: No.

Amount: _____   Cheque No. _____

To: _____   Acc. No: _____

School/unit: _____

Purpose: _____

_____

_____

Approved by: ____   Received by: _____

Expense form A

Date: No.

Amount: _____   Cheque No. _____

To: _____   Acc. No: _____

School/unit: _____

Purpose: _____

_____

_____

Approved by: ____   Received by: _____

Income Form

No.

Date: _____

Amount: _____

Cash/Ch. _____

From: _____

School/unit: _____

Against /Purpose: _____

_____

_____

_____

_____

Approved: ___   Received: ___

Income Form

No.

Date: _____

Amount: _____

Cash/Ch. _____

From: _____

School/unit: _____

Against /Purpose: _____

_____

_____

_____

_____

Approved: ___   Received: ___

Daily Fee Summary/Book

Date	Receipt No.	Admission Fee	Tuition Fee	Annual /Student Fund	Extra Student Charges

Daily Fee Summary/Book

Date	Receipt No.	Admission Fee	Tuition Fee	Annual /Student Fund	Extra Student Charges

Receipt Voucher (Cash\Bank)				Receipt Voucher (Cash\Bank)			
Date : _____				Date : _____			
Payee : _____		Voucher No	1002	Payee : _____		Voucher No	1001
Rupees: _____		Cheque No.		Rupees: _____		Cheque No.	
Particulars	A\C No.	Debit	Credit	Particulars	A\C No.	Debit	Credit
Cash	100		x	Cash	100		x
Bank	105		x	Bank	105		x
To Student Registration Fee	800	x		To Student Registration Fee	800	x	
To Admission Fees	801	x		To Admission Fees	801	x	
To Tuition Fees	802	x		To Tuition Fees	802	x	
To Exam Fees	803	x		To Exam Fees	803	x	
To Misc. Charges	804	x		To Misc. Charges	804	x	
To Annual/Student Fund	805	x		To Annual/Student Fund	805	x	
To Income from Sales	806	x		To Income from Sales	806	x	
To Interest On Saving	807	x		To Interest On Saving	807	x	
To Interest on Investment	808	x		To Interest on Investment	808	x	
To Grants/Donations Congre	809	x		To Grants/Donations Congre	809	x	
To Grants/Donations DBE	810	x		To Grants/Donations DBE	810	x	
To Diocese Contribution	811	x		To Diocese Contribution	811	x	
To Other Donations	812	x		To Other Donations	812	x	
To Income from Org. Activities	813	x		To Income from Org. Activities	813	x	
To Other Income	814	x		To Other Income	814	x	
To Others	815	x		To Others	815	x	
Other	816	x		Other	816	x	
		x				x	
		x				x	
Total		0	0	Total		0	0

Prepared By   Approved By   Prepared By   Approved By

Payment Voucher (Cash\Bank)				Payment Voucher (Cash\Bank)			
Date : _____		Voucher No	2002	Date : _____		Voucher No	2001
Payee : _____				Payee : _____			
Rupees:		Cheque No.		Rupees:		Cheque No.	

Particulars	A\C No.	Debit	Credit	Particulars	A\C No.	Debit	Credit
Teachers' Salary	500		x	Teachers' Salary	500		x
Other Staff Salaries	501		x	Other Staff Salaries	501		x
Compulsory Contributions	502		x	Compulsory Contributions	502		x
Overtime Payment	503		x	Overtime Payment	503		x
Water/Electricity Expenses	506-7		x	Water/Electricity Expenses	506-7		x
Gas/Internet and Telephone	508-9		x	Gas/Internet and Telephone	508-9		x
Rent/Insurance/S.S. Charges	510-2		x	Rent/Insurance/S.S. Charges	510-2		x
Capital Building/Furniture	513-4		x	Capital Building/Furniture	513-4		x
Capital Equipment/Vehicle	515-16		x	Capital Equipment/Vehicle	515-16		x
Repairs Building/Furniture	517-8		x	Repairs Building/Furniture	517-8		x
Repairs Equipment/Vehicle	519-20		x	Repairs Equipment/Vehicle	519-20		x
Stationery and Printing Expenses	521		x	Stationery and Printing Expenses	521		x
Postage and Revenue Expenses	522		x	Postage and Revenue Expenses	522		x
Teaching Material	523		x	Teaching Material	523		x
Office Expenses	524		x	Office Expenses	524		x
Transportation Expenses	525		x	Transportation Expenses	525		x
Training /News paper	526-7		x	Training /News paper	526-7		x
Expense of Lab/Sports and Functions	528-9		x	Expense of Lab/Sports and Functions	528-9		x
Withholding Tax/Bank Charges	533-4		x	Withholding Tax/Bank Charges	533-4		x
Others			x	Others			x
Compulsory Contributions(Deductions)	502	x		Compulsory Contributions(Deductions)	502	x	
Cash/Bank	100/105	x		Cash/Bank	100/105	x	
Total		0	0	Total		0	0

Prepared By   Approved By   Prepared By   Approved By

Cash Book

	Receipts						Payments				
Date	Particulars	V.No.	A\C No.	Amount	Acc. Balance	Date	Particulars	V.No.	A\C No.	Amount	Acc. Balance
	Opening Balance				-						

Bank Book

	Receipts						Payments				
Date	Particulars	V.No.	A\C No.	Amount	Acc. Balance	Date	Particulars	V.No.	A\C No.	Amount	Acc. Balance
	Opening Balance				-						

Ledger							Ledger					
Date	Particulars	Vr. #	Debit	Credit	Dr. or Cr.	Balance	Date	Particulars	Vr. #	Debit	Credit	Dr. or Cr.	Balance
	Monthly Total		0	0				Monthly Total		0	0		

61

FINANCIAL STATEMENT D.B.E.

School Name: Enter School Name

School Number: Enter School Code

Month: **April**

Trial Balance

Account No.	Description	Opening balance		Current month		Closing balance	
		Debit	Credit	Debit	Credit	Debit	Credit
Fees and Student Contributions							
800	Students Registration Fees						
801	Admission Fees						
802	Tuition Fees						
803	Exam Fees						
804	Annual/Students Fund						
805	Misc Charges						
806	Income from Sales & Provided Services						
Financial Income							
807	Profit/Interest on Bank Accounts						
808	Profit/Interest on Investments						
Grants and Donations Received							
809	Institutions or Congregations						
810	DBE Contributions						
811	Diocese Contributions						
812	Other Donations						
Misc. Income							
813	Income from Organised Activities						
814	Other Income						
Staff Cost							
500	Teachers' Salaries (Gross Payments)						
501	Other Staff Salaries (Gross Payments)						
502	Compulsory Contributions						
503	Overtime Payments						
504	Gratuity Payments						
505	Others						
Utilities							
506	Electricity						
507	Water						
508	Gas						
509	Telephone/Internet						
Fixed Expenses							
510	Rent						
511	Insurance						
512	Special School Charges and Taxes						
Capital Expenditure							
513	Building						
514	Furniture & Fittings						
515	Equipment & Teaching Aids						
516	Motor Vehicles						
Repairs and Maintenance							
517	Building repairs						
518	Furniture & fittings						
519	Equipment & teaching aids						
520	Motor vehicles						
Admin. & Educational Exp.							
521	Stationary & Printing						
522	Postage & Revenue stamps						
523	Teaching Material						
524	Office Expenses						
525	Transport & Travelling						

526	Training & Courses						
527	Subscriptions of Newspapers, Magazines etc.						
528	Expenses of Lab, Library and Computer room						
529	Sports & Functions						
530	Legal Service Charges						
531	Miscellaneous Expenses						
532	Expenses of Sales and Services						
Financial Expenses							
533	Withholding Tax on Bank Profits/Interests						
534	Bank Charges						
Grants and Donations Paid							
535	Institutions or Congregations						
536	DBE Contributions						
537	Diocese Contributions						
538	Other Donations						
Current Assets							
100	Cash						
105	**Bank name here**						
106	**Bank name here**						
107	**Bank name here**						
108	**Bank name here**						
109	**Bank name here**						
110	**Bank name here**						
115	Term Deposits & Investments						
120	Account Receivables						
125	Stock						
Current Liabilities							
130	Account Payables						
135	Withholding Tax Payable						
140	Student Security Fee Payable						
145	Provident Fund Loan Repayments						
Capital							
	Own Capital						
Total (both sides should be equal)							

Debit and Credit Rules for Incomes, Expenses, Assets, Liabilities and Equity

✓ **Income(s):**

Income is generated => Credited and vice versa {Tuition Fee, Exam Fee, Sale of Forms, interest income etc.}

✓ **Expense(s):**

Expense is incurred => Debited and vice versa {Salary Payment, Stationery, Repairs, Legal fee etc.}

✓ **Asset(s):**

Asset is increased => Debited and vice versa {Cash in Hand and Bank, Loan paid etc.}

✓ **Liability:**

Liability is raised => Credited and vice versa {Student Security Fee, Loan Received, Tax deducted from Salaries etc.}

✓ **Equity:**

Liability is raised => Credited and vice versa {Cash invested by owner, surplus income generated from operations, etc.}

www.ingramcontent.com/pod-product-compliance
Lightning Source LLC
Chambersburg PA
CBHW081253180526
45170CB00007B/2413